BOY FROM BUCHENWALD

BOY FROM BUCHENWALD

THE TRUE STORY OF A HOLOCAUST SURVIVOR

ROBBIE WAISMAN

with Susan McClelland

BLOOMSBURY
CHILDREN'S BOOKS
NEW YORK LONDON OXFORD NEW DELHI SYDNEY

BLOOMSBURY CHILDREN'S BOOKS
Bloomsbury Publishing Inc., part of Bloomsbury Publishing Plc
1385 Broadway, New York, NY 10018

BLOOMSBURY, BLOOMSBURY CHILDREN'S BOOKS,
and the Diana logo are trademarks of Bloomsbury Publishing Plc

First published in the United States of America in May 2021
by Bloomsbury Children's Books
www.bloomsbury.com

This book is based on the author's personal experiences. In some cases, the names and
other identifying features of people, places, and events have changed in order to protect
the privacy of individuals. This is because this is not a book about the individuals he has
described, but one about his own experiences and how they have shaped his life.

Bloomsbury books may be purchased for business or promotional use.
For information on bulk purchases please contact Macmillan Corporate and Premium Sales
Department at specialmarkets@macmillan.com

Library of Congress Cataloging-in-Publication Data
Names: Waisman, Robert, author. | McClelland, Susan, author.
Title: Boy from Buchenwald / by Robert Waisman, and Susan McClelland.
Description: New York: Bloomsbury, 2021.
Summary: A powerful memoir by a Holocaust survivor who was deemed hopeless and the
rehabilitation center that gave him and other teen boys the chance to learn how to live again.
Identifiers: LCCN 2020040259
ISBN 978-1-5476-0600-9 (hardcover) • ISBN 978-1-5476-0601-6 (e-book)
Subjects: LCSH: Waisman, Robert, 1931—Juvenile literature. | Buchenwald (Concentration
camp)—Juvenile literature. | Ex-concentration camp inmates—Biography—Juvenile
literature. | Child concentration camp inmates—Germany—Biography—Juvenile literature. |
Jews—Poland—Biography—Juvenile literature. | Holocaust, Jewish (1939–1945)—Personal
narratives—Juvenile literature. | Holocaust survivors—Biography—Juvenile literature. |
Jewish refugees—Biography—Juvenile literature. | Jewish children in the Holocaust—
Juvenile literature.
Classification: LCC D805.5.B83 W35 2021 | DDC 940.53/18092 [B]—dc23
LC record available at https://lccn.loc.gov/2020040259

Book design by Vikki Sheatsley
Typeset by Westchester Publishing Services
Printed and bound in the U.S.A. by Berryville Graphics Inc., Berryville, Virginia
2 4 6 8 10 9 7 5 3 1

To find out more about our authors and books visit www.bloomsbury.com
and sign up for our newsletters.

To Gloria Waisman, the love of my life,
and to the memory of my family, who perished
under the Nazis.

Contents

BOY FROM BUCHENWALD

One of the first photographs of Romek Wajsman following liberation from the Buchenwald concentration camp. Taken in Écouis, France, sometime in July 1945.

Some of the boys of Buchenwald in France. Robbie is first from right in the second row, arm in arm with Abram "Abe" Chapnik.

Introduction

"I mention her name and the old pain returns. Forget her, you say? How can you forget a living human being?"

—*Sholem Aleichem*

I REMEMBER WHERE I come from.

Skarżysko-Kamienna, located in south-central Poland, lies in the valley of the Kamienna River. If you drew a circle around Warsaw, Lublin, Kraków, and Łódź, Skarżysko-Kamienna would almost be the central point. And that was, in fact, how Skarżysko-Kamienna was formed: in and around the railway station that linked these cities together. Skarżysko-Kamienna, while small, was known for its industries, particularly munitions that in 1939 employed more than 4,000 of Skarżysko-Kamienna's 19,000 people. *Państwowe Wytwórnie Uzbrojenia Fabrykę Amunicji*, or the National Armament Factory, made arms for the Polish Army. When the Nazis invaded Poland in September 1939, they confiscated the

1

factory and gave it to a German manufacturer, who renamed it Hugo Schneider Aktiengesellschaft (HASAG). Many of the Polish workers were fired, and Jews were forced to make munitions for the *Wehrmacht* for no pay.

Jews had been in Poland for more than a thousand years, living through periods when we were relatively free to times when we were persecuted. At the start of World War II, Poland had the largest Jewish population of any country in the world. About 2,500 Jews lived in Skarżysko-Kamienna. Our community of Jews was called a shtetl. In all of Poland there were more than three million Jews living in many shtetls. The largest concentration of Jews in Poland was in Warsaw.

When my papa bought our house in the early 1920s on Maya Tziejo, which translates to "Third of May Street" in English, the Jewish communities in Poland were relatively accepted and lived in peace. Under Polish leader Józef Piłsudski, Jews had rights. Jews could own land and businesses and hold positions in politics, the military, and in universities. Skarżysko-Kamienna flourished in the first few decades of the twentieth century and attracted a lot of Jewish immigrants, including Papa, who came from Russia. The first synagogue in Skarżysko-Kamienna was built in 1910. A few years later, the Jewish cemetery was erected.

In 1935 Piłsudski died. Things weren't the same after that. I didn't know much of this back when I lived in Poland, though. To me, Skarżysko-Kamienna was forests and birdsong; winds that carried the warm, smoky aromas from our chimney; and cooking fires and the scents of our mamas' borscht and beef briskets.

Papa was a haberdasher and tailor. That meant he made

hats, mostly the black hats called *shtreimel*, a very wide-brimmed fur hat that Jewish men in Skarżysko-Kamienna would wear, but also city hats. He made suits, too.

Papa, whose name was Chil, had a wide face and strong shoulders and stood about six feet tall, just like my older brothers Chaim, who was twenty-two in 1939, and Moishe, who was seventeen. My two other brothers, Motel, fifteen, and Abram, twelve, were slowly stretching up toward them, too. And there was one girl, my sister, Rachella, who we all called Leah. She was eight years older than me.

While Papa's presence was large, his voice was soft. He was well-liked by everyone. The elders of Skarżysko-Kamienna and visitors to our small town would come to our home to hear Papa recite passages from the Torah; tell stories like *Tevye the Dairyman*; and seek his advice on politics, religion, and philosophy. Most of all, Papa adored Mama, whose name was Rifka. He would hold her hand when they would walk along the river, while I ran alongside them, trying to catch butterflies and skip stones in the water in the summer. In winter, I would skate on the river, looking up to see Mama and Papa still holding hands, still walking, but this time huddled close together underneath a knitted shawl draped across their shoulders.

To me, Mama and Papa and Skarżysko-Kamienna were love, laughter, and goodness.

I was born on February 2, 1931, and I was the baby of my family. Our house was small, made of wood, with a shingled roof. I shared a bed and a bedroom with two of my brothers.

Mama's cooking and quiet singing lulled me to sleep at night, but Papa's snores would often wake me up.

3

My brothers were strong, able to outrun everyone in town during cross-country races and soccer matches. My two oldest brothers were also handsome, so handsome that all the girls would swoon. Even as a child, I could see and understand—the girls' blushing cheeks, the way they turned a toe inward and bent a knee, their heads slightly cocked to one side whenever one of my brothers passed. I was so proud to be part of my family. I knew I was going to grow up to be just like my brothers, especially Moishe, who had applied to university to study engineering. He liked to tinker with wires and was making a radio that he said would be able to reach all the way to America. I wanted to be an engineer, too.

Mama always had chicken soup warming on the top of the coal oven ready for me when I would come in from chores. I helped Papa, sweeping up the fabric pieces scattered on the floor of his shop and holding his measuring tapes and devices while he fitted customers. I was responsible for carrying the wood to the woodshed, too, which my brothers would chop. I also gathered kindling from the forests for fires and swept the walkway to the street that led into the main center of Skarżysko-Kamienna where there was a cinema, my favorite place to go.

Oh, we had great dinners at our house. My family, as well as various guests, would sit at the long oak table Papa had carved himself, sipping wine from glasses that Mama would bring out for only such occasions. When the conversations turned serious about what was happening politically in Poland, the females would leave the men and my older brothers to themselves. My Jewish community was very conservative. Even at synagogue, the women would sit in the balcony while the men would be on the main floor.

One of my fondest memories was when my brother Chaim married Golda, the most beautiful woman I had ever seen. She had jet-black curly hair, one curl of which would flop down on her forehead like an upside-down question mark. Golda's hands were slender and fine, and she would dance around the room when she sang Yiddish folk songs or told stories. She reminded me of a swan. I had a crush on Golda. I wanted her for myself and even asked Papa if one day when the *schadchen*, a marriage broker, went to arrange my marriage, my bride could be Golda. But I was just a child, and Chaim was a man. He had finished his mandatory two years in the Polish Army and had kept on as an officer while he worked various odd jobs, like building fences and repairing homes. Chaim could offer Golda more than I could, Papa told me. I sighed and choked back tears, but I eventually became happy enough with the idea that Golda would always be in my life as Chaim's wife.

At their wedding, I ate and ate—challah, gefilte fish, cabbage rolls, and stewed chicken. I then danced the hora, around and around, before breaking away to eat some more, only to pass out from fatigue at the table, my head sinking down into a bowl of sweetened fruit and *smetana*. When I woke up, the bangs of my hair sticky from the honey, everyone was dancing outside in the back garden. So I leaped right back up and joined in.

When I looked to the sky, it was like the stars were dancing along with everyone.

———

Between the fall of 1939 and spring of 1945, I forgot these memories. And when I finally started to remember, they came

5

to me only in fragments, bits and pieces, like the fabrics Mama had collected to sew into her quilts.

On September 1, 1939, the German military, mder the German führer, Adolf Hitler, and his Nazi Party, invaded Poland. It took a little more than a month for the *Wehrmacht*, the German military, to take over the country.

The Nazis stripped us Jews of all rights.

In 1941, my family and I were forced out of our home and moved to a Jewish Quarter, which most people call today a ghetto. Skarżysko-Kamienna became the very opposite of love and, with the darkness folding in around us, I forgot where I came from.

I kept so much hidden, locked away in some vault inside me. I guess I had to.

My good friend Dr. Robert Krell, a retired psychiatrist, who was a hidden Jewish child during the Holocaust, said to me once, "When you're in survival mode, do you think you have the luxury of memory?"

For years, while still just a child, I lived minute to minute, not sure whether the guard standing nearby was about to kill me. I didn't know from where my next scrap of food would come, if it would come at all. I didn't know who I could trust and who would be the man—or child—to betray me. So many times I was slated for death, and each time I narrowly missed the fate of so many others.

I decided to start telling my story in 1984, when a man named James Keegstra, a schoolteacher in Alberta, Canada, told his students that what happened to me, that horrible period of our human history that came to be known as the Holocaust or, as Jews refer to it in Hebrew, the Shoah, didn't happen.

6

From 1939 until 1945, of Europe's more than nine million Jews, an estimated six million, including one and a half million children, were killed by the Germans, often in barbaric, cruel ways, including gas chambers and brutal medical experiments. Nazis tortured and mass murdered us. A whopping 90 percent of Poland's Jews were dead by 1945. Some died by walking into the electrical fences that surrounded the camps where we were imprisoned. They had given up.

I was there. I am a child survivor of the Holocaust.

I was a worker mostly, a slave laborer in a munitions factory making guns for the German soldiers during much of the Holocaust and then, when the war turned against the Germans, shunted in cattle cars from Poland into Germany, ending up at the Buchenwald concentration camp outside Weimar, Germany. On April 11, 1945, the American Army came and set me free. I wasn't alone. At that camp, hidden among 21,000 surviving prisoners, were 1,000 boys just like me.

I began to speak about this, at first quietly and hesitantly. Then I gained confidence and spoke to the media across North America, then Europe, and eventually as far away as Australia. I even spoke in Germany.

And an interesting thing happened along the way. I began to see that the Holocaust wasn't all I needed to talk about.

Slowly, like Mama would weave fine threads to embroider her linens, I found there was another story inside me. And forgive me. I am eighty-nine at the time of telling this narrative to my coauthor, Susan McClelland. I may confuse timelines and occasionally combine two characters into one. But the themes, our transition, how we boys who had lost everything found meaning again, are all true. How were we able to go on, many of us to lead extraordinary lives as doctors, lawyers, spiritual leaders, professors, teachers, parents, loving husbands, and doting grandfathers? Not all of us, mind you. Some died young and some struggled deeply with their mental and physical health issues. But the majority of us Buchenwald Boys went on to lead very fulfilling lives. Among us there was Elie Wiesel, whose writing and activism earned him the 1986 Nobel Peace Prize. He was one of us, the Buchenwald Boys, as we were dubbed by the press.

In the concentration camps, which we called "death camps," the men would whisper in the night, "If any of you live, you must tell the story of what happened here. The world can never forget. The world must never repeat what is happening."

Something else we can't forget is that love is stronger than hate.

And, as I discovered, love leads us home.

1

And wild animals shall meet with hyenas; the wild goat shall cry to his fellow; indeed, there the night bird settles and finds for herself a resting place.

—*Isaiah 34:14*

THE MAN WORE a crisp, clean, and long piped blue coat with brass buttons, a red swastika and medals, which I came to learn indicated his rank with the *Schutzstaffel*, also known as the SS, a paramilitary unit of the German Nazi Party. The man's sky-blue eyes were narrowed, his forehead furrowed, and he was pointing at me.

I was marching with the men to the munitions factory in Skarżysko-Kamienna, Poland. The factory was named Hugo Schneider Aktiengesellschaft Metallwarenfabrik but everyone called it HASAG.

I worked at the factory, as did thousands of Jews. All of us were slave laborers. None of us was paid. My job was stamping the initials FES onto artillery shells for the *Wehrmacht*. I could stamp 3,200 shells in each of my twelve-hour shifts, which I worked six days a week. When I started at HASAG, I was eleven years old. The year was 1942. For the first few months, I was working so hard, the skin on my hands chafed so much, that I bled. But if I stopped working, I knew—I had seen the Nazis and the soldiers from other armies who worked for them do it to others—I would be shot dead. I worked until the wounds became calluses that hardened like shoe leather.

I usually worked the day shift, which started at seven AM. But every few weeks, I was on the night shift, too.

As I marched along with the men on my shift, I lifted my knees up high, hoping to show the SS man that I was healthy. But the SS man nonetheless waved at me to step out of line. He was shouting, *"Raus!"* which means "get out" in German. The German language actually wasn't very different from Yiddish, which I spoke with my family at home. So I knew German words, at least a few, when I started at HASAG. By the end of World War II, I could pretty well speak German fluently.

I swallowed the lump that had formed in the back of my throat and did what the SS man said. He walked toward me, stopping so closely, I could feel his sticky, warm breath on my face. I smelled his breakfast of eggs and onions when he bent down to shout at me again: *"Raus!"* He then spun me around and dug the butt of his rifle in between my shoulder blades.

"March," he then ordered.

I pinched my eyes shut, knowing exactly where he was

leading me: to the pickup truck idling outside the front gate of the barracks where we slave laborers were imprisoned when we were not working.

I knew why I had been selected, too. For a fortnight, I had been drifting in and out of sweats and chills from typhoid fever. When my fever had broken and I discovered I was still alive, I suspected one of the men in the barracks, perhaps Papa's friend the kosher butcher, had kept me hidden under straw and given me water. You see, Lithuanian guards who worked for the Nazis came at seven AM and seven PM, when the night-shift men and the day-shift men traded places, making sure no one was hiding in the barracks or sick. Somehow, I had not been discovered.

As we neared the pickup truck, I opened my eyes. "Another one," the SS man spat to the men guarding the truck.

The SS man then ordered me to climb into the cargo bed. There were about twenty other men there, skeleton thin, their skin blue from malnutrition, many with scabs on their faces from the various diseases that flowed through the barracks the way the Kamienna River flowed through Skarżysko-Kamienna. There were some men whose skin was yellow: the slave laborers who worked with picric acid, an explosive related to TNT. Picric acid turned these workers' skin and eyes yellow and eventually destroyed their kidneys.

I knew we were being taken into the forest to be killed. First, though, we would have to dig our own graves.

"Another rat," I heard one of the guards say.

"Worm food."

I shivered with fear. I felt urine dripping down my leg.

11

I knew I had risked going back to work when I was still pale and slow-moving. But I had no choice. If I hadn't, eventually my absence would have been noticed.

When my brother Abram worked at HASAG alongside me, he would pinch my cheeks before morning roll call so I looked well and would place cardboard in the soles of my shoes so I appeared taller and older. The Nazis didn't really like children working, and they sent many away, likely to their deaths.

I was sitting in the cargo bed of the truck, at the very rear, staring out, first at the barracks—long, gray, and black—then the sky above them that moved like smoke. My eyes caught a cloud, traveling faster than the others. It looked like an island in the midst of a stormy sea. Suddenly, the shaking, the tremor that had dug itself right down deep into my bones, stopped.

I could see light, like the rays of sun, which, looking back, had to be impossible on that day.

I felt something wrap around me then, like a soft blanket, bringing with it a calmness, a lightness that I hadn't felt in the last three years, since before the Germans stormed their way into Poland, occupying it, making it theirs.

I was going to die, but suddenly it didn't matter.

I started to remember things I had forgotten since I started at HASAG: Mama singing me "My Little Town Belz," Papa wrapping me inside his *tallit* at synagogue, playing soccer with my older brothers. I even heard the voice of my sister, Leah, telling me we would meet again.

That dark island cloud then turned into wings, like that of one of the angels. *Azrael*, I mouthed. I could feel Azrael, the angel that transports souls to heaven, folding me, ever so softly, into himself.

Flooding me were memories of love that I knew would stay with me wherever I went.

I no longer clung to life.

I heard mystical sounds of wind chimes and tiny bells, even a chorus of singers.

I exhaled, knowing my breath was leaving.

I was in such a state of beauty and wonderment that I didn't feel at first the strong hand that had clasped onto the collar of my jacket.

I was being lifted off the truck.

The German man, the one who often came to HASAG to oversee the Jewish slave workers, the one I was sure held a high position with the Nazis, because the Germans would stand up straight, click their heels, salute him, and call out "Heil Hitler" when he walked by, this man was removing me from the truck. When Germans from Germany would visit the factory, he would show me off, commenting on how quickly and efficiently I worked. He was shouting at the SS man with the gun that I was too valuable a worker, that I worked faster than two grown men put together. I needed some time to get better. I had to be saved.

The soft music stopped and Mama and Papa disappeared.

Azrael was gone, too, the sky dark gray, spitting out rain.

Joe Dzuibek, from Łódź, Poland, writes on the side of the train, "Where are our Parents? Buchenwald orphans."

2

JUNE 7, 1945

"To forget the dead would be akin to killing them a second time."

—*Elie Wiesel*

THE TRAIN CAME to a sudden halt, shaking me awake.

I rubbed my eyes and looked out the window. Clouds slipped in front of the sun's rays, casting long shadows over what seemed like endless miles of wheat fields. My left hand, which had been tucked underneath my leg, was numb. I flicked it until I felt life return and then reached up and undid the window clasp. Abram Chapnik, whom I called Abe, was sitting across from me. He leaped up, and he and I leaned out and breathed in the fresh French air.

We both fell quiet, listening to the morning calls of sparrows, a raven caw in the distance, and cows mooing to one another.

I closed my eyes and tilted my face up toward the sky.

"Look," Abe shouted. "Hey, look!" He kicked my ankle hard.

"Ouch," I cried out, my eyes popping open.

Instinctively I had my fists balled, ready to punch.

The last time I had clocked Abe was back at the Buchenwald concentration camp, just as spring was inhaling its first breaths. At night, a biting wind moved in through the holes in the walls of our barracks. Above us were the groans and hums of airplanes. "American warplanes," whispered Yakov Nikivirov, also known as Jakow Goftman. Jakow was a performer with the Moscow circus or the Bolshoi Theatre—I was never sure which one—and he had taken Abe and me under his wing. Jakow told Abe and me the day before, "The Americans are near and dropping their bombs on Weimar." Some members of the underground movement at Buchenwald, Jakow went on to tell us, had climbed onto the roofs of barracks buried deep in the camp and spelled out SOS with white kitchen plates stolen from the Nazis to warn the American planes not to drop their bombs on us.

Weimar, which was about five miles away, was being hit hard. Buchenwald prisoners were being sent into the city after the American night bombing raids to clean up the rubble of destroyed buildings that littered the streets. Everyone clamored to go because the Weimar residents often handed out food. Abe and I had gone a couple of times. The first time, a German woman gave me half a loaf of bread; the second time, Abe and I were given some cheese and a bottle of milk.

Jakow was huge, like a giant to a giant, and wore a

mustache that curled at the ends. Jakow told us about the camp and the political prisoners, like Wilhelm Hammann, who was the Blockleiter, *leader of Block 8, our barracks. Abe and I called him Tall Willy, even though he wasn't very tall at all. Tall Willy had been a teacher, a member of the German Communist Party, a town councilor and then member of parliament for the province of Hesse. The leader of the Nazi Party, Führer Adolf Hitler, was a fascist, which meant he was a dictator. The Communists, Jakow told Abe and me, believed everyone was equal. The Communists were the very opposite of fascism. Tall Willy, like lots of other Communists, had been in prison since the Nazis took power in Germany in 1933.*

On the night of this particular American airplane bombing campaign, Abe was imitating the sound of the planes and then POW, KAPOW, the explosions. All of us kids in my barrack and the men were silent, except for Abe.

Jakow hissed at Abe to shut it.

Block 8 was near the front gate to Buchenwald. We were one of the closest buildings to the Nazi guards and not far from the buildings where the SS slept. We all knew the war was ending. Germany had lost. The Communists in the camp had access to information, and Jakow had told us that the Allied armies of Great Britain and America and a whole bunch of other countries were pounding on Germany's door to the west, and the Red Army of the Soviet Union was coming from the east.

All the prisoners in the camp were acting on their best behavior, terrified of drawing attention to themselves. Since they were about to lose the war, the Nazis might retaliate by killing us all, setting dynamite throughout the camp or send-ing us on marches with no breaks, until our knees gave way and we crumpled dead to the ground. There was also a rumor that the Nazis had disguised some of their own Luftwaffe bombers as American planes. When it was absolutely clear that the war was over, these planes would bomb Buchenwald, making it seem to the outside world that the Americans had killed innocent people.

But Abe wouldn't stop making airplane noises and put-ting us all at risk. As he became more animated, I belted him in the eye and then nose.

———

And I would punch Abe again, on the train.

"Leave me alone," I snapped, rubbing my sore ankle.

Abe tilted his head and batted his long eyelashes that framed large, dark-chocolatey eyes, which drooped in the corners, making him always look sad.

"What do you want me to see?" I said with a sigh, the ten-sion in my hands releasing.

Abe leaned out the window and pointed up the track. A group of men was headed toward us. Smoke from their cigarettes curled into the air. They wore black or blue berets. As they neared, I could see their weathered faces and clothes. These men were farmers, and they were speaking to one another in a language I hadn't heard before. "French," Abe whispered, reading my mind. "They're Frenchmen."

The men were gesturing toward the train. One French-man, with chiseled, high cheekbones and jet-black hair, locked eyes with mine. His face was red and his eyes fiery.

He hurled words toward me that I didn't know. I became breathless, and my lungs suddenly hurt. I felt I was going to faint. I spun around to get my bearings, feeling like the sides of the train were moving in around me.

I didn't smell the countryside, not anymore, but human waste and rot, body odor, blood and vomit. I wasn't on the train to France but one from Częstochowa, Poland, to Germany. Hundreds of us Jews were crowded into train carriages used for transporting cows and horses. In the wooden carriers that had no seats, no carpeting, no insulation or warmth, we were packed so tightly, we had little room to even turn around, let alone sit.

We went without food or water, sometimes for as long as five days. When the train stopped, which it did frequently, to allow trains with munitions and war supplies through, guards with guns would open the doors and demand we give them those who had died. The older Jewish men would recite the Kaddish, the prayer for the dead, as the bodies were handed down—no one able to shut the eyes of those who had died, as was Jewish custom—and then we'd all exhale a bit because we had more room to move.

"Snap out of it," Abe was shouting. I felt the palms of his hands tapping my cheeks. I coughed and then took big gulps of air, realizing I had temporarily passed out and possibly stopped breathing. With my eyes still closed, I reached blindly for Abe's hand and squeezed tight. As I did so, Abe whispered in my ear a prayer in Yiddish: "Lord our God, God of the Universe. Hear our prayer and listen to us . . ."

I was just about calm, starting to open my eyes, when I heard thumping against the sides of the train. I glanced out the window and saw the Frenchmen were throwing rocks at us now. One, about the size of a goose egg, flew in through our open window and banged its way up against the far wall. I quickly burrowed back down into my seat, curling my legs into my chest. I placed my hands over my ears to block out the sounds.

I reached up and tugged on Abe's shirt to tell him to sit down.

"Stop it," he snapped. "The French people just don't know who we are because of our clothes. It's going to be all right."

I patted my shirt and shorts. After the Americans came to Buchenwald, some soldiers had asked the Communists in the camp to find us boys new clothes. There were nearly a thousand of us boys, and all of us wore concentration-camp pajamas that were full of lice and could be carriers of other insects, including fleas that transmitted typhus. Someone found a storage room full of Nazi Youth uniforms and shoes and boots. There weren't enough uniforms for all of us boys, but for many of us, including me, we replaced our pajamas, which likely had belonged before us to people now dead, with clothes that had once belonged to killers.

"Look," Abe shout-whispered. "You have to look."

I inched my way back up to the window. Two of the Buchenwald Boys and Rabbi Robert Marcus, a chaplain with the American Army who was accompanying us, were talking to the Frenchmen. "Romek, we're not in danger," Abe said.

"The French are more afraid of us than we are of them. They hate the Nazis. The rabbi is explaining who we are."

I relaxed and listened as a quiet fell over the train. The French language sounded like a river with the occasional rise, like a crescendo in a symphony.

As I sat back down again, an older boy, short but not stocky like Abe, with knobby, scuffed knees, moved into our carriage. He pressed his body down into the seat on the other side of me. Without waiting to be asked, the guy started to explain what Abe had just told me. I guessed from his Polish dialect that he was from Kraków or Łódź. He was maybe sixteen, but it was hard to tell.

Abe pulled me up by the sleeve again. Along with the new boy, we peered out as the Frenchmen laughed and shook the boys' and the rabbi's hands. Now Frenchwomen, carrying wicker baskets bulging with food, smiled as they made their way toward the train. There were 427 of us Buchenwald Boys on the train that stretched to eight or nine carriages. A children's aid charity that, I later learned, was called Œuvre de Secours aux Enfants, which everyone referred to as simply the OSE, had arranged for us to leave Buchenwald. We were going to France, but another group, a smaller group on another train, was headed to Switzerland. Our train comprised the youngest boys from Buchenwald, and we all seemed to be clamoring to stick our arms out as the women distributed bottles of goat's and cow's milk, breadsticks, apples, and peaches.

After a while, the train started moving again, pulling into a side track near Metz in Northeastern France. Rabbi Marcus walked up and down the train, explaining that we would spend the night here, for our safety, until we could properly identify for the French who we were and who we were not: Nazis.

During the night, some of the boys used white paint a farmer had given them and wrote on the sides of the train in French, English, and Yiddish:

We are survivors from Buchenwald.
Where are our parents?
We are Buchenwald orphans.

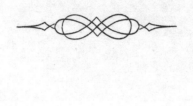

The boys arriving in France, wearing Nazi Youth uniforms.

3

AS THE TRAIN snaked its way across France, the new boy introduced himself to Abe and me as Salek, Salek Rothschilde. He was sixteen, he said, or at least that's what he figured. He, like most of us, wasn't keeping track of time. Salek was spindly, like a sapling, and those knees of his seemed to clank together when he moved.

Abe and I didn't know there were other boys beyond our own barracks at Buchenwald until the Americans came. Many of the thousand or so boys were hidden in Block 66, known as *Kinderblock*, which was deep inside the camp that was like a huge city, bigger than any one I had ever seen. Abe and I didn't even know how big Buchenwald was until liberation, when we drifted apart for what felt like a week, just wandering, like everyone else, in and out of the maze of buildings, sleeping wherever we grew tired. It was then that I saw there were hundreds of boys just like me. But I hadn't seen Salek before.

The Frenchwomen returned in the morning with more

peaches, bread, and sugar cubes for our breakfast. As I ate, it became pretty clear that Salek was a know-it-all, talking with his mouth full about the various French resistance movements that helped the Allies land on the continent, liberate France from German occupation, and eventually overthrow the Nazis altogether. Germany occupied France from 1940 until 1944, replacing French flags with Nazi swastikas and imposing strict rules on the press and media. Like in Poland, the French people were put on rations for food. Many went hungry. But France had a strong underground of resistance movements and spies, Salek was explaining.

"I betcha those farmers who thought we were Nazis were resistance guerrillas," Salek said, spitting crumbs of bread on his shirt as he spoke. "That's where a lot of the resistance took place—the countryside—with men like them blowing up bridges, stopping those German tanks and motorcycles. Stuff like that."

I started to tune Salek out, mostly because I was tired. After the Americans came, like our bodies had been storing illness, many of us boys got sick with chicken pox, measles, and other diseases. I had come down with typhoid for a second time, but this time I was nursed back to health by doctors and nurses with the 120th Evacuation Hospital and former inmates of the camp who had medical training. In a clinic set up at the camp, I had clean sheets; cool, fresh water to drink; and soup, as well as medication to help with the fevers and rash. But even after my treatment, I was still tired and slept for several hours during the day as well as right through the nights.

I soon fell into a fitful sleep, my rest punctured by the

movement of the train as it swayed through the hips of mountains. That's when, in between sleep and waking, the sounds of the fights on the train made their way toward me. Mostly it was just spitting words, sometimes in Polish or Yiddish, other times in languages I had picked up in bits and pieces from the camps: Hungarian, Russian, Lithuanian, and Ukrainian.

You see, for us boys, we didn't recognize that the war had ended. The way our illnesses drizzled out of us when we became free had delayed our ability to process our new reality. Now the war, for us, had just started, and we were fighting one another.

When I was working at the HASAG munitions factory, Jewish men at night would talk about how whoever survived had to tell the story of us, us Jews. However, Jakow told a different story. He warned Abe and me that if we got out of Buchenwald, we needed to be careful—very careful. "The ultimate victory of our oppressors is when we fight each other," he had said. "When abuse becomes all we know, we become abusers, hating ourselves and each other." And that's what we kids were doing now. The Hungarians were fighting the Poles, the Poles the Romanians, Russians, Ukrainians, and so on. But I couldn't stop that, either the urge inside me to take part or the others.

Western journalists wrote about us boys, languishing at Buchenwald weeks after liberation, most of us still sleeping in the very barracks where we'd been imprisoned, spending our days stealing from Weimar families and shops, vandalizing homes and public buildings and trying to kill one another. I heard murmurs around the camp that the Westerners thought we were misfits and psychopaths, a word I didn't know then but came to understand meant someone with antisocial behavior and a lack of empathy. We were all angry and full of rage, us boys. We didn't know the full picture of what had happened to the Jews in Europe. Most of us expected to go home but were told we couldn't. *"Les enfants terribles de Buchenwald* (the terrible children of Buchenwald)" was one newspaper headline. A group of psychiatrists who met us said none of us would live beyond the age of forty. We were too damaged, they said. Some journalists even wrote that we Buchenwald Boys had to be mean-spirited, tough, and unruly, aggressive and manipulative to have survived when so many others didn't. But the OSE, this organization that helped Jewish children, felt they could help us.

Physically we looked terrible, at least right after liberation. Little hair, faces and bodies sunken from hunger, our skin gray. All of us were full of mistrust and suspicion. A story about another American Army man named Rabbi Shachter, who was in the first jeep to enter the gates of Buchenwald, made its way around the camp. Piled off to the side of the front metal gates were mountains of naked corpses, murdered Jews. The vehicle stopped, and the rabbi got out. He walked around the bodies, his hand on the gun on his hip belt. Like us boys, I guess, the Americans were always on edge, too. He then stopped, stunned, for blinking out at him were eyes, child eyes, large, bulging, as all of ours were. The child was seven-year-old Lulek. He had been hiding among the bodies, afraid to come out. The rabbi picked up little Lulek, tossed him in the air, laughing and then crying.

"How old are you?" Rabbi Shachter asked in Yiddish.

"I'm older than you," Lulek replied.

"Why do you say that?"

"Because you laugh and cry. And I don't do either. So tell me who is older. Me or you?"

One of the reasons we Buchenwald Boys didn't get along, or so Jakow told Abe and me, was that Gustav Schiller, the deputy head of Block 66, had favored kids from his own country, Poland. Gustav was nicknamed the Executioner. He was part of the underground resistance movement at the camp. He was head of the Punishment Squad. When trains arrived, he and this large Ukrainian Communist named Otto would encourage new arrivals to identify those who had been mean in the ghettos or colluded with the Nazis. Not long after, these people would be found dead: smothered, rumor had it, by Otto in their sleep with a shirt or blanket or drowned in one of the latrines. Gustav apparently hated the Hungarians, even the kids, claiming that their country only entered the war in 1944, sitting back and watching us Poles suffer and die.

I was thinking of Jakow and Tall Willy as I slowly woke.

Abe and Salek were still asleep, their legs stretched out, their mouths ajar. Abe drooled, and Salek snored. I looked out the window. The train was speeding through small towns, some of which looked destroyed, with homes half bombed out, others with their frames sinking into rubble. I didn't know geography, just enough that I was moving away from and not toward Poland.

"We're not far from Écouis," Salek said. I jumped. I didn't know he was awake. Salek rattled on some more about the war in France, which he said destroyed entire cities.

I, however, was thinking of Poland, trying to remember what I could of where I came from, which was hard. Memories came to me fleetingly or in dreams, none of which I was sure was real. I did remember that throughout my working at HASAG, then on the trains and in the camps, I had a vision, a dream. I had started telling myself that it all was a test, like the way Chaim did exercises with the Polish Army. Chaim had told me he had to survive on very little food, in cold conditions, finding ways to keep his mind alert in very deprived circumstances, to fight his enemies. In my mind, I had a vision of my walking into our house. Papa, Mama, Chaim, Moishe, Motel, Abram, and Leah would all be sitting around the table, waiting for me. My mother, eyes alight, would stand up and cheer: "The baby made it!"

Abe was now awake, too. As the train slowed, pulling into a station, the sounds of shouts and screams, bouncing off the cement of the platforms, deafened me.

The train's center platform was crowded with people: young children, hunched-over elderly, babies in mothers' arms, babies in prams, men in suits. Everyone who could was waving.

Piling off the train was like being sucked up in a vacuum.

I lost sight of Salek as we merged with the other boys, descending the steps onto the platform. Out on the platform, I held my eyes tight to the back of Abe until he folded himself into the crowd, too.

I spun around and around, hoping to see someone, anyone, one of us or the rabbi. Someone I recognized.

Young Frenchwomen were clamoring onto the train, draping their arms around boys as they tried to disembark, while photographers snapped their pictures. Most of us boys, compared to the brightness of the French, were moody and glum, like rain clouds rolling in on a family picnic. A few of us were attempting to smile, but most looked as dazed as I felt.

I started to perspire. The back of my neck was soon drenched. I began walking toward what I thought was an exit.

As I pushed through the throng of people, the flashes of camera bulbs blinding me, the French thrust candies into my hands and bouquets of gardenias and daisies into my arms. I couldn't understand. I couldn't make sense of why we were so welcomed. I had spent the past five years being thought of as, well, not human.

When I finally made it outside, into daylight, I stumbled toward some grass, separating myself from the others, breathless and confused, not sure where I was or even if I was still alive. Maybe this was Azrael's way of welcoming me to heaven. Again I thought I was dead.

I braced myself against a poplar tree, bent over at the waist, vomiting, and then slipped to the dry ground, where I passed out.

Romek in Écouis, France, summer 1945.

4

"KID," WHISPERED THE boy with the mane of golden hair that flowed past his shoulders and was a bird's-nest mess. "Dance for us, Jew boy. Dance!"

My stomach churned. The soldiers patrolling the woods were going to hear us: the whoops, hollers, the gunshots staccatoing the air. German and Polish police, Papa had told me, spent their nights in the forests looking to shoot partisans and runaway Jews. We were both these things.

"SHUSH," I mouthed, raising a finger to my quivering lips.

The yellow-headed kid pointed his pistol at me. "Dance, Jew boy." He chewed the words out through his wine-stained teeth.

He and his posse of partisans—a military movement aimed at ousting the Germans from Poland—were sitting in a semicircle around a blazing fire that probably could have been seen all the way in Kraków.

The older boys, almost men, were all drunk, slurring their words, purring, singing, screaming. They were drunk on stolen alcohol, including beer, vodka, and wine, which I helped them loot earlier in the night from the homes of Polish farmers or Jews forced from their houses into the ghetto.

When the boys were not drinking, they moved through the forests near the town of Bliżyn hunting for squirrels to roast and eat and guns to use against the Nazis.

About a month earlier, Papa had bribed a guard at the HASAG barracks with Mama's wedding ring to let me escape under the electric fence. During the few moments in between guard shifts, the electricity was turned off.

Papa had given me instructions to go east, find Białowieża Forest and Jewish partisans. Białowieża Forest was a sea of thick woods, where people could disappear for an entire life. But I didn't make it that far before I bumped into this particular group of Polish partisans.

For the first few weeks I was with them, the leaders were kind. They gave me food and a new pair of shoes. They gave me a cause: subvert the Nazis. But they never disclosed their plans to me. I was getting the sense they really didn't have any plans. All I saw was a bunch of renegade older teenagers.

After a few weeks, they started to see me as entertainment. I was the Jew boy.

"Dance. Dance. Dance . . . Jew boy," the yellow-haired boy shouted again. The others had fallen quiet, their heads down, perhaps sensing that this was now going too far.

A light layer of snow covered the ground. Snow that was melting into mud that looked like Mama's chocolate puddings.

The partisan was forcing me to dance because he wanted to see if I could move fast enough to escape the bullets he sprayed near my feet.

I was a game to him. His sport.

I leaped from foot to foot, exhausted, but moving quickly with the energy of fear. Tears dripped down my cheeks.

At one point, he raised his pistol, no longer aiming at my feet but at my heart and then head.

He was going to kill me.

I could see it in his eyes.

I woke up panting, choking for air.

Panicked, I quickly patted my face, then stomach, thighs, and feet, eventually letting out a long exhale that all my parts were there and I was still alive. I was no longer in the forest with the partisans. I was in a dorm room in France.

As my breathing slowly returned to normal and I started to relax, I looked around the room. When we'd arrived, OSE staff said they were going to leave all the lights on in the buildings because so many of us boys had nightmares, for in the darkness, we remembered the camps, the ghettos, the trains . . . and in my case, also the partisans.

My clothes, for like most of the boys, I was still sleeping in my Nazi Youth uniform, were stuck to my body with sweat, my shirt twisted from my restless night. My bedsheet, for we had these now, was lying disheveled on the floor, likely from my having kicked it off during the night. But at least I had bedding. Back in the camps, before Buchenwald, I was lucky to have a blanket, and even when I did, I would have to share, and it would be filled with moth holes and rat bite marks.

After I had vomited and rejoined the group, we boys left the train station and were taken to an abandoned sanatorium, a place where the sick went to get better. There was one main building, the largest house I had ever seen, where we ate in a long dining hall and where meetings took place with psychologists and therapists who had us doing art and playing music. We also did physical exercises out on the lawn. The property held smaller, one-story buildings, where we boys slept, sending shivers through not just me but Abe and Salek, too, because they reminded us of the barracks at Buchenwald. Although here, in Écouis, our bunk beds had mattresses and only one person to one bed, not six or seven of us.

My building, which had been divided into two sides separated by a curtain, held about twelve of us between the ages of fourteen and sixteen. Salek, Abe, and I were on the same side.

A dull gray light stretched its way under the window blinds.

I could hear swallows and goldfinches waking up outside, then a rooster call.

My eyes scanned the room and the silhouettes of sleeping, snoring, mumbling boys, tossing and turning like I had. We all had places we visited when night came. None of us escaped that. Nights, I had first discovered back in the ghetto, were the toughest to endure. Night was when the *dybbuks*, the spirits of displaced souls, got in, Jakow had told me. The wailing, crying, shaking . . . tears of people unsure whether this night would be their last. "Nights open doors cemented shut by day," Jakow had said. We Jews bled hope in the night as the voices in our heads ripped out of us whatever we had spent the days hiding. Nights should have been what bound us boys together, I thought for a moment.

The room stank almost as badly as the cattle trains had. None of us felt like showering or brushing our teeth. I didn't even clean my hands after going to the washroom or before eating. Dirt was caked under my fingernails.

When we had arrived at the Écouis complex, staff explained that we were under quarantine for a month, which meant we were not allowed to leave the property. The French government apparently didn't trust that we weren't bringing diseases into France that French citizens could catch, and so for thirty days, we had to stay put. OSE staff showed us the various bathrooms. In the main house, the washrooms were large, with smooth white ceramic floor tiling. There were these cow trough–like contraptions that Salek said were bath-tubs, which could fit a grown man the size of Jakow. These bathtubs sat on metal legs painted to match the white ceramic toilets and bidets, which were French devices, Salek further explained, to clean our private parts. I'd never seen a bath-room before, not like these. In Skarżysko-Kamienna, we had an outhouse made of stripped wood. Our toilet was a hole in the ground. And we washed ourselves in tin buckets. In the camps, we had outhouses, too, except the floors were usually covered with urine and excrement.

Abe, sleeping in the bunk above me, groaned and then farted. I stifled a laugh.

I slowly slid my legs over the side of my cot and then slipped my shoes off so I wouldn't make any noise when I walked. Most of us slept with our shoes or boots on. We got used to that in the camps, too.

I was glad I was one of the first awake. I didn't want to see anybody, especially the Hungarian guy with scars on his face. He didn't speak Polish, German, or Yiddish, and I didn't know Hungarian. When he found himself in our room, he rushed to fighting with us Polish boys. Salek was already nursing a bruise on his cheek from the Hungarian guy's elbow that had narrowly missed his eye.

I tiptoed toward the front of the building and slowly opened the door. Outside, I put my shoes back on.

As I made my way to the main building, I inhaled the aromas of brewing coffee and baking bread. I realized then that I was hungry, very hungry.

When I moved to open the door of the main building, a hand thumped down on my shoulder, pulling me backward. I sped around on my heels, my hands balled and ready to punch.

It was only Salek. "What do you want?" I said with a huff, lowering my fists. Salek had folded himself into Abe and me, like we were now a threesome with him as boss.

"You're going to look for the list," he said. It wasn't a question. He was referring to the list the Red Cross was compiling of Jews who had survived. Many of the survivors were getting documented at displaced-persons camps being set up across Europe.

"You're going to find the list, right?" Salek repeated. "Let's go together." He linked an arm through mine. I shook it away. Not only was this guy now my self-designated leader, it bothered me that of us hundreds of boys, he always seemed to be, not so much happy but eager, like some fire in his belly was keeping him moving all the time.

My feet were not moving. I studied him hard. I didn't want to see the list. My family were safe back in Poland. I'd be going home soon. But for some reason, I couldn't push out the words.

"I'd like to be alone," I eventually said with a sigh.

From out of nowhere, I remembered that I used to love mornings back in Skarżysko-Kamienna. I would go out into the back garden and listen to the sound of silence in the winter snows. Occasionally, the white landscape would be blotted by a cardinal. In the summers, amid the haze that would flirt up around me like a dance, I'd listen to the chickadees and chase butterflies. On Sundays in Skarżysko-Kamienna, and after regular Polish school during the weekdays, I'd go to *cheder*. *Cheder* was Jewish school, where I learned the Hebrew alphabet and the Torah. I was just starting to learn Jewish history and parts of the Talmud when Germany invaded Poland. It wasn't long after that the Nazis banned Jewish children from going to school and decreed that Jewish schools and ceremonies were illegal.

"When quarantine ends, Lulek and his older brother Naphtali are leaving Écouis for Palestine," I caught Salek saying as I walked into the building.

I made my way to the kitchen with Salek, who was ignoring my request to be alone, in tow, led by the sounds of clattering plates and the lively chatter of French cooks.

"Lulek and Naphtali are famous." Salek never seemed to stop talking, and his mind was like an encyclopedia of facts that I had no clue how he developed, since like me, he'd been out of school for years. "Those journalists who would come to Buchenwald always asked to speak to Lulek and the really young ones, because of their stories," Salek was still saying. "The journalists were amazed they survived, you know." I knew Lulek's story, but Salek proceeded to tell it to me anyway—how Naphtali had carried Lulek into Buchenwald hidden in a potato sack. Naphtali didn't want the Nazis to know about Lulek, fearing he was too little, that he would be killed after the first selection. When it turned out that the underground at Buchenwald was in charge of selections, at least the ones right off the train on arrival, and protecting us kids, Lulek came to his older brother's aid, having him transferred to a barracks where he, too, would be safe from the Nazis.

"I'm not planning on ever moving away from Europe," I said. "I'll be returning to Poland soon and reunited with my family." There, I said it.

"Okay," Salek said with a shrug. "Okay," he said, raising his hands, imitating a surrender.

When Salek and I entered the dining room, Madame Rachel Minc, who was in charge of the lists but also recited poetry to us at night, was reading the story of Moses and his exodus from Egypt to a few of the boys who couldn't sleep. Little Lulek was sitting on her lap.

Abe had now joined us, and he and Salek were talking, loud enough for Madame Minc to pause her story and look over at us, about ditching the day's programs to go in search of some of the pretty French girls they'd seen at the train station when we arrived. Abe and Salek headed toward a long table near one of the large windows in the room. Abe said he wanted to get there first and fast and at the ready because as soon as the OSE staff set food on the tables, hands would fly, taking everything in sight. That's the funny thing about hunger. now that we had food, we hurried to eat and ate too much, fearful it would run out again.

I had fallen back from the others, moving a little slower, when a voice moved up beside me. "Even in the darkness, it's possible to see light." The voice was soothing, romantic, almost a lullaby. I knew that voice from Buchenwald. It belonged to Eliezer, a Romanian Jew or Hungarian Jew (his shtetl in Sighet was located in a geographical area where one day it was part of Romania, the next Hungary). We all referred to him as Elie.

Elie fascinated me. He and his band of friends, which included Naphtali and by extension little Lulek, I referred to in my head as *the Intellectuals* because they talked philosophy and religion and did math and science. They were religiously devout and had asked OSE staff for kosher food. They wanted to do Shabbat, Jewish sabbath, which back in Skarżysko-Kamienna started in midafternoon on Fridays with the closing of all Jewish shops. Jews go to synagogue during Shabbat, read parts of the Torah, and pray. We have three special meals during Shabbat, starting on Friday night, too.

Not all the boys wanted to return to our religion so quickly.

I stopped and looked into Elie's long, drawn face. "What?" I murmured. Now, if Salek carried himself like a sapling, Elie was like a withering spruce tree.

"We always have a choice to choose light or dark," he continued. I shook my head slowly. The rest of us stank,

41

belched, and fought. We didn't make much eye contact, especially with OSE staff; didn't listen to them; and moved around the property skittishly, like prisoners waiting to return to their jails. And here was this guy among us who spoke in metaphors, like he really wasn't one of us at all.

Elie smiled and, mysterious as he was, breezed past me toward a table near the front of the room that in the evenings, when the tables were pushed to the side and the chairs arranged like a theater, was a stage where string quartets and opera singers performed. I watched Elie move, his gait so smooth, like he was floating, almost like a specter, his feet not touching the ground.

"Grab food," Abe called out. I looked over. Abe and Salek were standing, stuffing into their mouths at the same time as their shirt and pants pockets bread they'd ripped off from the long loaves, pieces of cheese, apples, walnuts, and apricots. "We'll be out all day, hunting bullfrogs," he called with a full mouth.

Since we had arrived, most of the boys and I were hoarding food, often under our pillows, including pieces of cake that we wrapped in napkins and got squished. I certainly didn't trust OSE staff when they said we could eat whatever we liked and whenever we liked. The OSE even assured us the kitchen would never be locked. I rolled my eyes when I heard that.

I darted beside Abe and grabbed some bread that I quickly buttered, swallowed a few large pieces while barely chewing, and then ate some foul-smelling cheese that I immediately spat out. To wash away the bad taste of the cheese, which Salek said was called Camembert, I popped into my mouth three hard-boiled eggs at the same time, my cheeks bulging like a squirrel's.

Satisfied we had enough food, Abe and I, and our growing posse that included Salek and two other Polish boys, Joe and Marek, started making our way to leave. As we wove through the dining hall, my gaze floated back to Elie. Starting when I worked at the munitions factory, I was able to fine-tune my eavesdropping skills, which I had first learned in my home when the elders would gather with Papa and my older brothers to talk about the war. By hiding myself in tiny places or pretending to do something else, I'd hear a lot. With Elie, I knew he and his father had been in Auschwitz, a concentration camp. Elie's papa had died just after they arrived in Buchenwald.

I wasn't paying attention to the others in the room and felt a whomp on the back of my head. I rubbed my scalp. A dove-egg-size lump started to bubble up. On the ground in front of me swirled a chipped cereal bowl. I spun around and saw the Hungarian boy from our dorm winking at me from across the room.

"He threw that!" I hollered to no one in particular.

"Come on," Salek said, doing what he did best—taking control—yanking me down to the floor. He and Abe grabbed the food from the table and then pulled the table on its side so it formed a barricade, scattering the white linen, china, and cutlery.

Behind the barricade, I reached for some plates, hurling them one after the other, the way I did skipping stones on the Kamienna river. They missed the Hungarian boy but hit other kids who then joined in the war.

All of a sudden, tables were being turned over across the room. The food, however, was always protected. Us boys never messed with food.

Cutlery and dishes crisscrossed in the air. I guessed it wasn't just me, because that stinky Camembert cheese was being tossed against the walls, where it stuck and slipped slowly down to the floor, leaving grease stains on the white paint.

We were fighting one country against another. Jew against Jew. Hate against hate.

With every toss, I cursed. In my mind, I was aiming to kill my enemies—every Nazi who had made me afraid, terrified, horrified.

"Pow, pow," I cried out like Abe, pretending my plate throwing was actually a rifle shot. Dishes and plates were even being thrown out the open windows.

I hurled a saucer so hard, so precisely, seeing it move so fast through the air until it landed, skipping along the floor, coming to rest in front of a man, Professor Manfred Reingwitz, one of the counselors with the OSE. The professor was watching the saucer, too, until it came to rest by his feet. He then looked up and glared at me. "Come with me," he said.

———

"Leave me alone," I spat as the professor dragged me by my shirt collar across the floor.

His hands smelled of pipe tobacco and cologne. He wasn't a big man, and he wore, even in the summer heat, a tweed jacket and long woolen slacks. But despite his lack of size and seeming clothing restrictions, he was strong.

I reached up to try and pry loose his fingers but couldn't.

He pulled me out of the dining room and along the hallway toward Madame Minc's office. I managed to use her doorframe to propel my legs around so I could kick the professor in the shin. But he still didn't let go. With a superpower strength, he heaved me up and tossed me into a chair in front of Madame Minc's desk.

As I sat back with a huff, I snarled at him. I wanted him to fight me. I was angry that he was so calm.

The professor was not an old man, younger than Papa but older than Chaim. He definitely looked posh, like those Jews who would come to Papa's shop from the big cities, Kraków and Warsaw. The professor, Salek's theory was, had been holed up in some art gallery like the Louvre, where the Nazis stole a lot of the artwork. "He looks cultured, like he knows Cézanne and Monet." Salek had beamed. "They're famous painters, in case you didn't know." The only painters I knew were Chaim and his army friends, who painted houses and fences back in Skarżysko-Kamienna.

One thing was for sure: there was no way the professor knew anything about what we boys had gone through.

Madame Minc entered the room, her face fresh not flushed, her expression belying the fact that outside her office, a battle in the dining room was raging. Looking at her made me angry, too, because her hair was a mop of dark curls, like Golda's. I didn't want anyone to look like Golda.

I hissed when she looked at me, then looked away.

For the longest while, the professor and Madame Minc didn't say a word.

I listened to the boys in the dining hall yelling and swearing and the sounds of breaking ceramic plates and cutlery.

"Romek," Madame Minc finally said in a soft voice. I breathed heavily.

"Romek," she repeated. I closed my eyes and hummed one of the Buchenwald underground songs, the "Peat Bog Soldiers."

For us, there is no complaining,
Winter will in time be past . . .

"Romek, listen to me," she said. I heard her push back her chair and move in front of me. I then felt her gently touching my chin and swiveling my head until I was looking into her face.

"Romek, we found your sister. We found her. She's in Germany at a Red Cross camp."

Jakow Goftman.

5

MADAME MINC HELD up a piece of paper.

I knew it was *the list*.

I stared at the writing—black ink on white paper.

I saw some letters I recognized, but then everything went blurry. My insides froze and melted at the same time.

"Romek, do you remember how to read?" Madame Minc asked, sensing what was wrong.

"No," I wanted to tell her. No. My last completed grade was four. I was nine when I stopped going to school. I was now fourteen. In the ghetto, a rabbi had organized a secret *cheder,* held in the basement of his apartment building, buried underneath cement so that the guards, including the Jewish police on the streets, wouldn't hear. Chaim had told me that the rabbi could be killed if word got out he was teaching us Jewish prayers and stories. But that was it, all my schooling for the past five years.

"There," Madame Minc said, pointing to a name on the list. "Rachella Leah Wajsman. Born in Skarżysko-Kamienna,

49

daughter of Rifka and Chil, sister of Romek. That's you, correct?"

I nodded, my eyes blurring and focusing, blurring and focusing.

I finally looked up, staring at a yellow stain on the white stucco ceiling. "Where . . . where is she?" I stammered, my pulse racing.

"In Feldafing. South of Munich. In Bavaria, Germany," she said. "Feldafing used to be a summer camp for Nazi Youth. The Americans turned it into a camp for displaced persons."

"Can I go?" My voice was shaky, my throat parched. I felt like I was going to vomit.

"Not until quarantine ends. You also need proper identification, which we are organizing for everyone."

"I want to go now," I said. It was slowly registering— Leah was alive. This was the start. Soon I would be reunited with everyone. "I can't wait." I stood up then, ringing my hands together.

"You have to," Madame Minc said. I could sense the professor moving in close. "Foremost, you have to get new clothes." I felt the professor lay a hand on my shoulder. "You can't go back to Germany wearing those." Madame Minc was referring to my Nazi Youth uniform. "For one, you could be killed. Nazis right now are being rounded up and beaten, tortured, even killed by other Germans who never supported them."

The professor lifted his hand away and passed me a glass of water. With a shaking hand, I took a long sip. Everything around us was now quiet. The boys' battle had ended. I could hear the ticking of the large grandfather clock in the foyer.

"Nathan," I whispered, placing the glass of water down on the desk. I watched condensation begin to spread out from underneath the bottom of the glass, staining the wood, and caught Madame Minc looking, too. She didn't move to give me a coaster. "My nephew," I pressed on, lifting my hands to my face. "Golda and Chaim's son. He was in the barn with me." I don't know what came over me or where it came from, but like the condensation out of the glass, the story of Nathan swelled out of me.

"When Chaim heard rumors that the Nazis were going to round up everyone in the ghetto and send them to camps, he took Nathan and me away."

Nathan and I hid on the floor of Chaim's truck, underneath a thick sheet he used for painting. Chaim had a truck from HASAG, I think, where he worked. Chaim begged me not to make a sound, to keep Nathan quiet by giving him butterscotch candies. I felt the truck moving, then stop. I heard Chaim talking to one of the guards and the ruffling of papers, probably his identity card saying he worked at HASAG. Then I felt the truck move out of Skarżysko-Kamienna. When Chaim said I could look up, I saw that we were in the countryside, parked near a barn. Before we got out of the truck, Chaim told me that I had to hide in the hay until he returned. He then handed me more candies for Nathan, saying we couldn't make a sound. No one must know we were there. "We stayed, Nathan and me, in that barn for an entire night and day. My legs became sore and cramped. But I whispered in Nathan's ear stories from *cheder* and stroked his back until he fell asleep. Then Chaim came, taking Nathan but not me.

"Nathan," I said, looking up at Madame Minc. "I need to

find Nathan. I need to make sure he is safe. I need to get him."

"Romek," Madame Minc finally cut in. She was now kneeling in front of me. "Romek, it's best we not talk about what you've been through . . . what all the boys have been through. It's time to look to a future again. Do you know what a future is? What do you want for the future?"

I tilted my head and stared at her, realizing that what I really wanted more than anything was to tell this woman with the wild hair, this woman who reminded me of Golda, I wanted to tell her my story. I wanted to remember all the things I had forgotten.

Instead, I took a deep breath, then grunted that I didn't care about my future. "Isn't that what all of you think of us anyway? We're not right in the head. That we don't have futures!"

"That's not true," Madame Minc and the professor said at the same time. But by then I was halfway out the door, set on a mission to find Salek and Abe, to skip the programs and hunt bullfrogs.

———

I found Abe and Salek, Marek and Joe sitting cross-legged underneath one of the drooping weeping willow trees on the property.

I sat down in the middle of them. In turns, they ruffled my hair and chided that they had been waiting for me. "Finally," Abe said, punching me on the shoulder, "the staff is doing something about your bad behavior," stressing "your," like I was the one responsible for all the fighting.

"It was nothing like that," I mumbled, but I also didn't tell them about finding Leah, mostly because I was a bit in shock. Leah was supposed to be at home in Poland with the others, waiting for me.

The OSE staff, since we boys had arrived, had done nothing about our bad conduct, which included taking the laundry—sheets and linens—from the lines and wearing it over our clothing as togas, soiling it in mud and grass stains. Some of the older boys snuck off into Paris, despite quarantine. Most of us didn't pay much attention to the speakers they brought in, except of course the Intellectuals. It was now sort of an unsaid competition among us boys to see who could get the staff to react first. The boy who got in trouble would be given an imaginary badge of honor.

The five of us set off down a dirt path that eventually led out into a field.

We leaped over a broken part of a stone wall and headed into the countryside.

We walked through pastures of goldenrod and dandelions and then slipped into a meadow, until we landed back out on a dirt road. Then we walked stealthily, quietly, until we found another path leading us into a forest. We ran, then, hard, racing against one another, taking off our shirts mid-stride and tying them around our waists. We were still all stick thin, little muscle to show for anything, but we could set a pace I wanted to imagine would rival Jesse Owens, the African American runner whom Jakow had told Abe and me about at Buchenwald. Jesse Owens had shamed Adolf Hitler by winning four gold medals in the 1936 Olympics in Berlin. We didn't have a radio in Skarżysko-Kamienna, so I'd known nothing about Jesse Owens until Buchenwald.

The path joined up with another dirt road, lined with

daisies and lavender, evergreen trees and pussy willows. Salek reminded us not to wander off the roads because, like the northern beaches of France, there might be land mines. But none of us seemed to care. What was death anyway when we had already died.

Pretending to be American Army men, we found sticks we posed in our arms as weapons and pretended we were hunting Nazis. We twisted and meandered, crossing streams by hopping over rocks and tiptoeing across decaying tree trunks covered in blue-green lichen and moss that we pretended were bridges.

We found cherry trees and raspberry bushes, our fingertips bubbling in bruises and blood from the thorns, and ate until our tongues turned red. With our bellies swollen with fruit, Abe and Salek turned to play, using the slingshots they had made from the insides of old tires. They aimed at wood pigeons and anything that moved in the forest.

We finally came out in a clearing and rested on a long, flat rock. Abe and Marek built a fire pit in the middle of it. Salek and I found some dry wood and, with some matches Abe brought along, made a fire, where we toasted the bread we had taken at breakfast.

After, we all became still, watching the flames.

In the quiet, my mind drifted to the train from Częstochowa, Poland, to Buchenwald, when the cattle car had room for us to sit down and stretch because many of the people who had started off with us had died. A man on the train had gotten ahold of a can of meat. He had no way to open it, so he made a fire on the floor of the train. He stuck the can in the middle of the flames, hoping the heat would burst the lid.

I had moved in close to warm myself, because it being January, it was freezing, and all I had to wear were my concentration-camp pajamas. The can exploded. Burning meat splattered across my face. I screamed. I thought I had been blinded. The pain, the physical pain, was the worst I had ever experienced. I wanted to die. I turned to the other boy on the train, a scrappy kid named Abe, and told him to take the lid of the can and jab it into the vein in my neck so I would bleed to death. That's how Abe and I became close. He refused to kill me.

I was sure, though, that when I arrived at Buchenwald, I would be selected for death. My face, even though Abe and the men on the train downplayed it, was burned. I could feel the swelling around my eyes and cheeks and the rawness of the wounds. The Nazis would view me as sick and unable to work.

At the camp, after registration, Abe and I were led to a series of large circular bins that contained milky water that I overheard another prisoner say was disinfectant to kill all the lice. After taking off my clothes, I was ordered to get in.

I sat in the metal basin, legs curled up, shaking and breathing heavily, convinced that when the guard took a good look at my face, I'd be shot. The guard, wearing a blue uniform with a black beret, approached. He looked right into my eyes. This was it. Using a long stick shaped like an SS baton, he pushed me down, submerging my entire body in the liquid.

He was drowning me.

The pain of the disinfectant on my facial burns pulsed through me. I bit my lip so hard to stop myself from screaming, I could taste blood.

But then I felt the pressure of the baton lift. I floated to the surface. I looked around. The guard was wandering to the next basin to check on the prisoner there.

Had I skirted death again?

That disinfectant ended up saving my life, because it was so strong that it cauterized my wounds. My face began to heal almost immediately.

———

Back out on the road, crows circled overhead, seeming to squawk directly at us boys.

After an hour or so of walking, yelling, swearing, and killing stuff—mostly by stomping on beetles and snails, as none of us had great aim with the slingshot—we found ourselves entering a town. The houses were small, like those in Skarżysko-Kamienna, and had chipped paint, broken cement, and falling-down fences. One house had scaffolding holding up one of its sides. "The war between the Allies and the Germans was fought all around here," Salek said.

Joe, who wasn't much of a talker, said then that he wanted to be an army general, like George Patton or Walton Walker of the American Army. Both men had visited Buchenwald. "I want to make sure what happened to us . . . to this world doesn't ever happen again," Joe said in a low voice.

I studied the houses. Like eyes, houses, I felt, told stories. These houses, despite being run-down and war-bruised, contained light. Some houses just seemed happy.

"Maybe we can scare the French people by thinking the war has started all over again," Abe said. I looked over. He had put his Nazi Youth shirt back on and was marching like the German guards we'd seen at the camps: legs straight, back stiff, kicking out from the hips. Joe and Salek stripped right down to their underwear, wrapping their pants and shirts around their necks, saying in no way whatsoever did they want anything to do with these clothes. Abe and Salek then started a contest to see who could spit farther.

As we moved into the village, I spied some bikes lined up outside a shop. "What do you think?" I asked, eyeing a blue bike. Suddenly I remembered I'd had a blue bike. Papa had gotten it for me from a neighbor. It was too big for me. My feet couldn't reach the pedals. Until my legs grew longer, I sat astride the frame and pushed the bike with my legs. I wondered where that bike was now.

"Why not," Abe said slyly, slinking up to a small red bike, swinging his leg over the seat, and coasting it out onto the street.

Each of us took a bike. We pedaled fast, out of the village, up a hill, then down, at one point running right through a family of ducks crossing the road.

We rode for what seemed like hours, somehow managing to navigate ourselves back to the sanatorium. When we arrived, it was past dinnertime, twilight settling around us like a laced wedding veil. The music from a violin concerto floated over us. I wondered for a moment if it was the Hungarian boy playing. Not the one who wanted to beat up Abe and me but another boy, who had stolen a violin from Weimar after liberation. He'd walk around the camp playing for the Americans, and when we got on the train to France, having been ordered to leave behind everything we had stolen, this boy refused to be parted from his instrument.

We dumped the bikes behind a dovecote.

We five boys then headed to the far edges of the property, where we sat under that weeping willow tree and ate the rest of whatever food we had stored.

We sat, saying not much at all to one another, until it was pitch-dark, the crickets serenading us with their night songs.

The boys in Écouis.

6

"Whose burnt and barren brick, whose charred stones
  reveal
The open mouths of such wounds, that no mending
Shall ever mend, nor healing ever heal . . ."

Russian Jewish poet Hayyim Nahman Bialik

MY BOYS AND I were still hungry, so we made our way to the main building to raid the kitchen.

When I stepped into the house, one of the Polish boys from my dorm said Madame Minc had been looking for me.

Abe cooed that I was in for it now. Salek motioned to meet them in the dining hall after.

Madame Minc had me sit in that big armchair again. She moved behind her desk and rummaged through some stacks of papers.

"Found it!" she announced, sinking into her chair, which matched mine.

My back stiffened and my mouth went dry, thinking, *It!* It had to be my ticket to Feldafing.

"You know Elie?" she began instead. I nodded.

"He is writing about his experiences," Madame Minc said, catching my eye. She didn't blink. For a moment, I wondered if we were holding a contest to see who would look away first. It ended up being me.

"I know we're encouraging you boys not to speak about the past, for your own good, to help you move on, but maybe . . ." Madame Minc pushed a book, a pencil, an eraser, and a pencil sharpener across her desk. I flipped open the book. It contained blank pages.

"What's this for?" I asked.

"The professor wondered if maybe you might want to write about what you've been through, like Elie. He wonders if maybe we have it wrong and it might actually be therapeutic, healthy, to talk about what you've been through." Her voice was strained, as if the subject of telling stories frightened her.

I said nothing, my mind a stew of thoughts, none of which I could catch, all of which made me feel clammy and nervous.

"I know you're smart," Madame Minc continued. "I can tell. You will progress very fast and far once you return to school. Maybe, in the meantime, draw pictures of the words you don't know. Tell your story in illustrations, any way you can."

I said nothing.

"I'd like to see you go to school," she pressed on.

"I don't think so," I murmured. School? What was school? I needed to get back to Poland to my family.

"Okay. We can talk about school when you're ready. In the meantime, try and draw your experiences . . . about Nathan," she then said, pushing the book, pencil, and eraser even closer to me.

I snapped at the mention of Nathan. My nostrils flared as I felt myself heating up. Beads of perspiration dripped down my forehead, and I was balling my fists. Nathan, I wanted to scream at her, was mine, one of the only things I still had, still owned—my story and memory of Nathan. "Don't mention Nathan's name again," I said in a gruff voice.

"Sorry. I'm only trying to help."

"I don't want your help," I murmured. "I'm going home to Poland."

She stood up and moved until she was in front of me. She put her hands on my shoulders as if she were going to hug me. I started to flinch. My body twitched. I hadn't been hugged since . . . when?

At the same time as I wanted to push her away, I found myself wanting to sink into Madame Minc's warm arms, the way I also remembered doing with Mama. I wanted Madame Minc to tell me everything would be all right.

"Romek, I need to tell you something."

I looked into her dewy eyes.

She swallowed before starting and took a deep breath. "Romek, you don't have a home to go back to," she whispered.

I tilted my head, indicating I didn't understand.

"Most of the Jewish homes in Poland, the Germans, well, they gave these homes to other families or just allowed non-Jewish families to take them over. We're hearing reports out of Poland of Jews returning to their houses and being killed by the new occupants. It's still very dangerous for Jews in Poland. Poland is now under the control of the Soviet Union. It's not safe. I think . . ." she trailed off.

My head started to spin. Running through my mind was that memory, that dream, the one that got me through the death camps, of running into my house and Mama announcing, "The baby's home." I was so sure that this image wasn't just a wish but real, a prophecy.

Madame Minc had to be wrong.

"I'm not wrong, Romek," she said softly. "I wish I were."

"If I had known that," I found myself mumbling after a long silence, "I would have given up. I would have . . ."

"I know, Romek." And for the first time, I felt, she really did know. She understood.

The door to Madame Minc's office swung open. One of the cooks announced there had been another fight.

I quickly swallowed everything back down that had been so close to coming out, reminding myself that I couldn't trust anyone, anyone at all.

———

I made my way back to my building, the book of plain paper, pencil, eraser, and sharpener tucked under an arm.

The other boys were still not back. The air was muggy. Out near that willow tree, I spied fireflies.

As I walked along the corridor of buildings, I caught, out of the corner of my eye, that there were pieces of paper tacked to the doors that hadn't been there before.

My pace slowed to a caterpillar crawl as I recognized some of the words. City names: Łódź, Budapest, and Warsaw.

"The staff felt that we would be better placed in rooms with others from the same city," I heard *that* voice say. Elie always seemed to sneak up on people. He moved out from a shadow and stood in front of me. He gave me a crooked smile.

"The staff felt that if we stayed in the rooms where we were from, rather than the rooms of boys our age, it might stop the fighting. What's that you've got?" he then asked, pointing at my book.

I grumbled that it was something to write in.

"I'm trying to write, too," he said as he started to move away from me.

"What are you writing?" I asked.

Elie stopped, turned, and spoke slowly, carefully, like he was searching for the right words. "Madmen and death . . . My father . . . The camps . . . ," he eventually said. "I write about what I can remember, not just up here," he said, tapping his head, "and not just what is in here," he added, rubbing a hand over his heart. "But what is in between, and all out there, and what connects the two."

I shook my head. Elie spoke in riddles, and I could never quite make out what his words meant.

"Do you like writing?" I asked. I couldn't quite explain it, but I liked his attention.

"Yes," he whispered, then added, "the OSE people are doing their best to cope with something they . . . the world . . . has never really had to deal with before. It's the first time, I think, they're going to try and rescue us, us kids, who have experienced the worst of humanity."

I remember things; they come to me in dreams and visions,

I wanted to tell him. "I feel guilty about something," I said instead. "I don't know what."

Elie studied me. "I think a lot of us feel guilty because we're alive when so many are not." He then said that he had heard rumors that some people believed we boys must have been ruthless, just bad kids, to have survived when others didn't. "But it's not true. I don't think there is much meaning at all in what has happened to us, our loved ones, our people. None of it makes sense. Guilt, I think, is trying to make sense of the insensible." He turned to leave again.

"My family is still alive," I said quickly.

Elie stopped again but this time did not turn back. He said nothing for the longest while.

"Good night, then," he eventually said over his shoulder.

"I don't even know if I can hold a pencil anymore," I called out as he rounded a corner.

———

I couldn't find Skarżysko-Kamienna on any door.

"You're in the building with the boys from Łódź," the Hungarian who wanted to beat me up said. I jumped, expecting that finding me alone, he would want to finally have that fistfight. But I saw tears in his eyes. "I guess you heard," he said in a choked voice, "about Poland, about being unable to go back." I nodded. As he passed me, our arms brushed. I leaped again, thinking he was going to punch me. "I am s-sorry," he stammered instead. "I'm really sorry."

I eventually found the building for the kids from Łódź.

Inside, my eyes scanned the bunk beds until I saw my unused toothbrush and soap on a dresser beside one of the cots. My rotting food had even been placed under the pillow.

I lay down on my bed and stared up at the wooden beams of the bunk on top of me. My throat was raw, my eyes fogging. Then it came. First as a whisper, then a wave, finally a downpour. Tears soaked my cheeks, shirt, and pillow, which I grabbed and clutched to my face to muffle my screams.

I cried and cried, weeping and wailing so hard, my voice soon became hoarse and then vanished altogether.

There was no going home.

There was no home, not anymore.

7

"Those who can make you believe absurdities can make you commit atrocities."

—*Voltaire*

FOR DAYS, I lay on that bottom bunk; at nights, in the bed above me was Marek, on the bed next to me Abe.

During the day, I had no energy or desire to go exploring with Abe, Salek, Joe, and Marek, who were heading out to the meadows and forests almost every day, swimming in the streams and racing across the wheat fields.

I just floated in and out of sleep until I wasn't sure whether I was awake or I was dreaming.

Madame Minc and other OSE staff came regularly to check on me, feeling my forehead and taking my temperature. I didn't have a fever. And when a doctor was brought in, he, too, said there was nothing physically wrong with me. "I think it is psychological," I heard him say to a staff member.

"Just let him be for a while. If in a week or so he is not better, we can decide next steps."

Someone fed me chicken soup, lifting the spoon to my lips in a way that reminded me of how Mama and Leah would do it when I was sick with a cold or flu. That memory sent shooting pain through me.

Leah, always Leah haunted my thoughts. *I need to get to her. If only the OSE would let me leave.*

The professor came, too, sitting on the corner of my bed and talking, talking about nothing at all, the weather I think, and the gardens outside, how so many of France's majestic flower gardens had been turned into vegetable patches when Germany occupied the country. There was little food, and the vegetables helped.

He talked about some famous jazz singer, Josephine Baker, who I gathered was American but who lived in France. She'd headed up or joined some resistance movement and was now even more famous. I think the professor said something about taking me to Paris to see her perform, to listen to jazz, a lot of which was influenced by African American army men from World War I who had stayed on in France. The professor had a feeling I would like jazz. That music, fine art, stories, and dance could float their way inside a person, make them forget the spinning and noises in their head and help them remember what was good and pure and real in this world.

I wasn't really listening. My world had been shattered. I would not be going back to Poland, and there was nothing, no dream inside me, to take its place.

But whether it was Madame Minc or the professor, when

they stood up to leave, I grabbed on to a piece of their clothing, begging to know if the train ticket had come yet for me to see Leah. "Is quarantine over so I can leave?" I would ask with a dry, parched mouth, my voice barely audible.

"Another week." The answer was always another week.

Abe or Salek, sometimes Marek, brought me bread and eggs, leaving a plate on the floor by my bed. I never ate. A couple of times they accompanied me to the bathroom. I knew enough to know why. They were scared I was going to do something to myself, like a few of the Buchenwald Boys did after liberation. They'd survived long enough to know they didn't want to live anymore, and like the men who would die walking into the electrical fences, they just let go of life.

"Don't you get it?" I wanted to scream at Abe and Salek. "If I die now, it will be over. My suffering will end." For some reason, I felt I deserved pain.

————

Papa was saying we wouldn't have to live very long in the ghetto.

"A few days," he told Mama. "Once the Germans high up hear what the soldiers are doing in Poland, they'll step in and stop it."

But the days turned into months, which turned into more than a year.

As time increased, our food rations became less and less. At one point, we Jews were allocated as little as two hundred calories a day per person. The price to buy extra food, like a loaf of bread or a few potatoes, smuggled into the ghetto and sold in makeshift markets, was one thousand times what it would usually cost, and no one had any money. The Nazis allowed each Jewish household only two hundred złoty a week and two thousand złoty in their bank accounts. If it wasn't for Chaim, who had a special permit to go in and out of the ghetto with his job as a driver for HASAG, we would have all gone hungry. He was picking up eggs for us and bread from Polish farmers trying to help. In the final months of the ghetto before it was shut down in October 1942, humanity, Motel would say, was out the window. Fathers took food away from starving children on the streets to feed their own families; Jewish police, chosen by the Nazis, controlled the makeshift markets and medicines, handing these needed supplies out to people they liked or to rich people who bribed them, in some cases becoming more brutal than their SS overlords. But Papa, Papa, he kept saying everything would be all right soon. "People will come to their senses soon," he would say.

It was never "all right" again.

When it was clear I wasn't getting out of bed anytime soon, the professor began to set a chair close to my bed and sat there, reading passages from *Tevye the Dairyman* by Solomon Rabinovitsh, more commonly known as Sholem Aleichem, a Jewish comedy writer. I liked it when the professor read. I started to pay attention.

I was thinking a lot about Papa during this time, what I could remember. When the professor read, I recalled that Papa used to tell me this story. My favorite part was when

Tevye's oldest daughter, Tzeitel, said she was going to marry her childhood sweetheart, Motel. Motel and Tzeitel broke tradition by not using a *schadchen*. I liked this because Motel and Tzeitel reminded me of true love.

On another day, when the boys returned to the dorm to sleep, I heard them talking about Gustav from Buchenwald. He had shown up at Écouis. He wanted to help the OSE staff with what he referred to as "his boys." The OSE staff loved the idea of having someone around who the boys knew and respected. And since Gustav's arrival, all the Polish kids who had been in Block 66 were looking to him for instruction. Instead of running into the dining hall and grabbing food the moment it was set on the table, they now walked, almost marched, sitting quietly until Gustav motioned for them to start eating. Abe said the Polish boys who had been in Block 66 were acting like they were still in Buchenwald.

Not everyone was happy about Gustav's arrival, though. The non-Polish boys wanted to turn him over to French police for the murders he'd committed at Buchenwald. I had missed a very unruly meeting, Abe told me, in which Gustav was booed by a group of boys and then cheered by the Poles. The divisions between us boys were deepening.

I had set eyes on Gustav only a few times in the camp and only after liberation. I heard that during the days leading up to liberation, he walked around Buchenwald with grenades in his pockets, looking for retreating SS. His plan, allegedly, was to detonate the grenades under their vehicles.

For the time being, Gustav could stay at Écouis, Abe told me, but Madame Minc and the other OSE staff had suggested we boys decide his fate by holding our own trial.

A week passed, as I wasted away in bed, my limbs listless, drifting in and out of dreams and sleep, nightmares, which I would awaken from in a cold sweat to the professor, who it seemed was always there, his face awash with concern. On the eighth day, though, something just switched inside me. I couldn't explain then or now, but I felt hungry. I ate an omelet with basil and rosemary, followed by half a loaf of bread and three peaches. The professor told me to slow down, that I might be sick. But I was famished. When I stretched my legs over the bed, my head swooned at first, and I faltered, gripping a dresser, as I tried to walk to the washroom.

When I returned, Professor Manfred seemed almost relieved at the turn in my illness. "You survived, Romek. Catch up on your schooling, move on with life. I will help you," he said. "Put all your sorrow aside, at least for now, and do something to make your parents proud."

I wasn't really listening to his words. I just knew somewhere in one of those nightmares, I chose life.

What also prompted me to get up was that sometime over the past week, I had devised a new strategy for surviving: if I wasn't going to Poland, meeting up with my family who would be waiting for me there, I would find them all in Europe. We would reunite and move to a new town, a new country maybe, a new house, a new life, together.

———

"He's a hero," said the boy, nearly a man, maybe a man, sitting on the floor in the corner of our room.

Salek, perched at the end of my bed, leaned over and

74

whispered that the man's name was Ralph, Ralph Lewin, from Łódź. Another Pole.

Ralph's long legs were curled up underneath him. His black hair was slicked back with some gel. He had large almond eyes that moved from boy to boy and then back again. His eyebrows were bushy, like the bushes that lined the country roads, but jet-black, like his cotton shirt and pants.

All the boys in our dorm were listening to him, some of the kids lying on their beds with their legs and arms draped over the sides, others on their stomachs on the floor with their elbows on the ground, their heads propped up in their hands.

"Joseph Stalin, the leader of the Soviet Union," Ralph continued. "He liberated us. He and his Russian troops ended the war. He is our savior. We should follow him!"

"I thought the Americans liberated us," I wanted to say, but everyone seemed to be entranced by this Ralph guy who looked maybe eighteen, possibly nineteen, so I figured maybe I was wrong. Salek leaned over again and explained to me in a hushed voice that Ralph had been at Buchenwald. Since he was older, he didn't have to come to Écouis. It was his choice, so he arrived on his own after traveling around Germany. Along with a few hundred other Buchenwald Boys, Salek whispered, Ralph had gone east to Poland and Russia. I knew that at Buchenwald there were arguments between Rabbi Shachter, who wanted us boys to go west to democratic countries, and the Communists in the camp, who were encouraging the older boys to return to their countries and help in the socialist movement.

"He's an activist . . . a Communist," Abe added. He was

sitting on the floor in front of me, his head bobbing up and down as Ralph spoke, like being an "activist" was a good thing.

"When are you going back in?" Joe called out. *In* being Germany, the front lines.

"I will go to Germany soon," announced Ralph. He gave off a similar air as Salek: a know-it-all, someone I didn't trust completely, but he also caught my interest. It wasn't just his charisma that seemed to mystify the other boys. Ralph was going to Germany, and I wanted to go with him.

"If you get photos taken of yourself, I'll bring them to the displaced-persons camps and hand them out," Ralph said. "After Germany, I am returning to Russia."

I propped myself up on an elbow. Now he really had me. I wanted to go with him to find Chaim. Chaim had said that once he knew all of us were safe, he would head to Russia to join other troops from the Polish Army who were training there. I'd pick up Leah at this place called Feldafing, then go to Russia and find Chaim. After that, we'd all go to Poland and first find Nathan, then the others.

"What's it like in Germany?" Marek asked, moving up close and crouching in front of Ralph.

"There are diseases everywhere. Jews are rotting in displaced-persons camps, needing food and medical care. Everyone, even the Germans, is hungry, as the war destroyed many of their crops and most countries won't trade with Germany now. But the Soviets, the Russians, they're doing their best to help." As Ralph talked, his arms flew around the room like he was giving a lecture. He was like Jakow at Buchenwald, when he'd tell stories about Russia and princesses and princes who lived in kingdoms made of diamonds and pearls. Jakow told his stories over several days.

"Look," Ralph said, rolling a cigarette. He had one already tucked behind each ear. Ralph dug out a small notebook and pen from his breast pocket. He then proceeded to draw what he said was a map of Écouis, marking with a dot the sanatorium. "There is a photography shop right here," he said, making a big X on his map. "Forget this stupid quarantine—go and get pictures made. Have the photographer create about a dozen or so prints that wherever I go, I can hand out, see if anyone recognizes you. Write your full names and birthdays on the back—if you can remember your birthdays—the names of as many relatives as will fit, even distant cousins, and the town in which you were born and lived. Maybe your relatives will recognize you instead of you waiting here, hoping to find them through the lists."

Ralph finally lit the cigarette he had been rolling and passed the ones behind his ears around for us boys to share. When it was my turn, I coughed. I'd never smoked before.

"Stalin is a prophet, a messiah, a dear Father, a man of steel," Ralph continued as he blew smoke rings. Now, he was an expert smoker.

"But what about Elijah and Moses?" Marek asked. "Our prophets?"

"Look at what our prophets got us: a history filled with persecution, pogroms, and now this mass murder," Ralph said with a moan as the room filled with a collective gasp. "Communism, Stalin's Communism . . . his way of thinking . . . ," Ralph continued, "Stalin has the answers you seek. With Communism, there's complete equality. Man, woman, gentile,

77

Jew, rich, and poor, all equal. The way God wanted, except . . ." He trailed off.

"Except what?" Abe and Salek probed. Like a magnet, Ralph's words pulled everyone in the room a bit closer.

"Except there is no God," Ralph said matter-of-factly. "Religion of any kind separates people, not unites them."

Another collective gasp filled the room; then everyone fell quiet. In the camps, there were prisoners who said God had abandoned us Jews. And then there were others who, despite the horrors, continued Shabbat as best they could and prayed. Our faith, said the Jewish brickmason who taught geography in Block 8, was one thing the Nazis couldn't take from us. "You can only give that away," he had said.

"But for many Jews, the Nazis did take away our beliefs . . . not just in our religion but in the trust and flow of life itself," I whispered, so low that no one could hear me.

"The gods of our camps were the Communists who looked after us," Salek eventually said in a weak voice. It was like his comment broke the collective inhale, and the room slowly filled with *aha*s and nods of agreement.

I sat up and swung my legs around so I was sitting facing Ralph. I put my hand in the air the way I would do in school. He looked at me and nodded. "The gods I saw at Buchenwald were Tall Willy and Jakow," I said in a meek voice, in part from having not spoken for more than a week, in part from nerves that I was saying something that was wrong, that I knew my family would never approve of. "These men were the ones watching out for us," I continued, though. "They saved us."

"Our gods were Antonin and Gustav," said one of the

78

boys who had been in Block 66. Antonin Kalinin was a Czech Communist who headed the block.

"And the brickmasons," another boy called out, referring to the two hundred or so Jewish brickmasons who had built Buchenwald and then were sent to Auschwitz. These men, mostly Polish Jews, had a skill the Germans needed and so hadn't feared death.

"To Gustav, Antonin, Tall Willy, Jakow, and the brickmasons!" Ralph shouted, raising a fist in the air.

Us boys pounded our feet and cheered along with Ralph.

"Stalin is our Father. To Stalin. Let's go defend our brother Gustav. Our brother, our brother, our savior."

8

"It's burning! Brothers, it's burning! God forbid, the moment may be coming when our city together with us will be gone in ash and flames, as after a battle—only empty, blank walls! And you stand there looking on with folded arms, and you stand there looking on—our town is burning!"

—*Mordechai Gebirtig, Yiddish folk song,*
"Our Town Is Burning"

MY BROTHER ABRAM *and I were working side by side in the munitions factory, twelve hours every day, Monday through Saturday. Sunday was the Christian day off, a holiday for the Germans, and so a day off for us slave laborers, too.*

On the other days, Abram and I would pass Papa as we marched to and from the HASAG factory. Papa never had the same shift as we did.

HASAG slave workers marched on roads littered with

corpses, which, for a while, Rabbi Yechiel Feldman would collect in a wheelbarrow and bury in the Jewish cemetery. Then the cemetery was destroyed by the Germans, and the rabbi went missing.

In the barracks where we were confined when not working, there were lice and bedbugs and rats. We bathed in a cow trough, cold water, unable to do much but slap our faces. We slept in the clothes we wore during the day.

During roll calls, in what the Germans called the Appellplatz and often taking place without warning, the SS would do selections. They would point to a prisoner and tell them to go "LEFT" or "RIGHT." One way meant life, another week of work; the other way meant disappearing, never to be seen or heard from again. Those who were sent away were quickly replaced with Jews trucked in from other liquidated ghettos, small towns across Poland, and eventually healthy working men and women from the Warsaw Ghetto—people to work in the factories until they became too weak from hunger or illness themselves.

Abram got typhoid before I did.

His skin was scalding hot. But he'd moan that he was chilled to the bone. His lips turned white and then cracked, and he was covered in a bubbling rash. I asked one of the men in the barracks if I could take my brother to the infirmary, which was close to the factory, that we would pass when we marched. I saw nurses through the windows, nurses wearing white uniforms.

The men in the barracks said the infirmary was for the Nazis and the soldiers working with them from other countries—Ukraine and Lithuania. So I hid Abram; we all hid him best we could.

The guards, who checked the barracks, found him.

I was at the Appellplatz one dawn before work, a fog rising up around us. I saw Abram being placed on the wooden cart used by guards to take away the sick and dying. I got out of line and followed, hoping Abram was being taken to see a doctor. Instead, I saw Abram being loaded onto the back of a pickup truck.

I screamed then and ran toward Abram. I screamed at the guards to let my brother go, that he was just ill. He would get better. I begged the guards to let him go. They laughed.

Then one of the guards smiled and told me Abram was going to the infirmary. But I could tell he was lying. I could see it in his eyes.

A man from my barracks whom I did not know came toward me. He pulled me into his arms and told the guard that he would look after me. "Forgive his outburst," the Jewish man repeated, bowing at the same time. The man held on tight as I struggled to get loose.

The man hissed in my ear to be quiet. To settle down. Or I would be in the back of the pickup truck, too.

I watched the truck move off down the road, disappearing around a curve.

The man eventually let go. When everyone from my shift had left the Appellplatz and gone to work, I hung back. I sat on a curb, my chin in my hands, sleet scratching at my face, waiting . . . waiting . . .

Until I heard the sound of gunshots echoing across the forest and making its way to the barracks.

When the truck returned, no one was on it.

Abram was gone.

I started to wail.

"All Abram ever did was help people," I shouted at the sky, the clouds, at Azrael. "What did he do? What did he do to deserve this?"

———

The tables in the dining room had been pushed to the side, similar to when the room was used for concerts and plays.

But unlike when the center was set up like a stage and hosted actors and musicians from Paris, it now had been arranged like a courtroom. Even the chairs had been placed not in semicircles around the performers but horizontally. On one side sat the Intellectuals, including their leader, a boy named Menashe Klein, and then there was Elie. There were also nonintellectuals on that side, too—boys from various countries except Poland. They were talking among themselves that Gustav needed to be turned over to French police because he was a criminal, a murderer. He was also a Socialist and France, with its long history of democracy, didn't like Socialists. I whispered to Abe that I hoped that side of the room didn't know about Ralph. On the Polish side were Gustav's supporters, claiming they were alive because of him and his underground network. I sat with my posse and the other boys from Poland.

Gustav sat front and center behind one of the long dining room tables. At Buchenwald, Gustav's hair, like most other prisoners, had been shaved. Now his hair was stretching down to his shoulders, and what shocked me most was that it was fiery red. Beside him sat Madame Minc, who had suggested this open trial, and on the other side of Gustav was an OSE staff person I had never seen before.

Madame Minc opened the trial by discussing Janusz Korczak, a Polish Jewish children's writer and philosopher, who wrote under the name Henryk Goldszmit. Many of the Poles in the room, including Salek, nodded. Salek leaned over and said the man was known as Pan Doktor or Mr. Doctor. Pan Doktor had a radio program in Poland and advocated for the rights of children. Pan Doktor spoke out against corporal punishment of children, which was common not just among Polish families, Salek said. Madame Minc was saying that Pan Doktor believed child development was optimal when children could play, express themselves, be taken seriously, be held, and be loved. He also founded an orphanage for children that operated inside the Warsaw Ghetto.

Even though Pan Doktor could have sought sanctuary, he remained with the children when they were among the first to be rounded up by the Nazi SS and sent to their deaths at Auschwitz-Birkenau. I knew this part of the story from Jakow. Legend had it, he had told me, that the children marched to the train station dressed in their best clothes, carrying blue knapsacks with their favorite toy or book inside. Pan Doktor told the children they were leaving the country and to be happy, even though he knew their fates. Rumor had it that even up to the last minute, in the gas chamber itself, Pan Doktor was urging the children to be joyful and happy. Madame Minc was saying that this trial of Gustav was based on Pan Doktor's teachings of giving power to children to decide for themselves Gustav's role in Buchenwald and whether he should remain with us.

The trial, or tribunal as a few of the boys were calling it, needed to have some order, so one of the older Polish boys led our side of the deliberations, while an Intellectual led the opposition. The so-called prosecution side, the other side, spoke first, outlining how, at Buchenwald, when there were extra blankets, mittens, food, Red Cross packages, or socks and shoes, Gustav would hand these out to the Polish children even though children from other countries may have needed these items more. Gustav would shove non-Polish boys out of food lines so Polish children could go before them. The Intellectual side also laid out how Gustav's job at Buchenwald, as head of the protection unit, was to murder prisoners who were found to have collaborated with the Nazis, were Jewish police or guards in ghettos, or treated other Jews with brutality. After the first boy spoke, the other boys added testimony, including one who said he saw one of the murders. The inmate had been smothered with a pillow.

Gustav, with his head lowered and eyes facing downward, just shrugged.

The Polish side championed Gustav, saying he helped build the schools in the children's barracks in the camp. He had organized the Jewish brickmasons to come in and teach them Jewish folk songs, tell stories, and do math and reading when they could. "You made me dream when all my dreams were nightmares," one boy recalled.

"I had wanted to run into the fence like the men I'd see, but you changed my mind," another said.

Our defense side talked about how Gustav and his underground risked their lives to save us.

The trial broke for dinner. The tables were pushed back.

The Intellectuals and their allies sat on one side to eat, the Polish boys on the other.

I was conflicted; on the one hand, learning Gustav had killed many people upset me. But on the other hand, he was a collaborator, and sure, he had killed, but he had saved many people, too. Most of all, I felt a familiarity with Gustav I didn't with the other staff. Maybe it was the knowledge he had been in hell with us. While I hadn't known Gustav at Buchenwald, he reminded me of Jakow and Tall Willy. I felt safe with him around.

The evening part of the tribunal ended up turning into a philosophical discussion with questions being asked like, "Where lies the boundary that no one must cross, lest he lose his soul?"

Finally, Gustav spoke, explaining how, when the trains would come, he and his squad with the protection unit would approach the prisoners and ask them who among them had cooperated with the Nazis. Few would come forward at first, all of us having it ingrained within us not to trust anyone. But eventually, the truth of some prisoners would come out and make its way back to the protection unit. Gustav said the camp held trials similar to our tribunal. But identifying Nazi sympathizers was the way to keep the underground operations and camp safe, and one of those operations involved saving us children. Even after a verdict was handed out, sentencing—which was usually death—was never carried out right away. A few days were allotted for any new evidence to be presented in support of the prisoner.

"We never killed for the sake of killing," Gustav said loudly. His voice echoed throughout the big dining hall.

Composing himself and sitting back down, Gustav went on to talk about how one prisoner, a doctor, was even allowed to live, although his crimes against Jews were horrendous. Five hundred Jews had been quarantined in a synagogue in his hometown. The SS had asked the doctor to see if the prisoners were in good enough health to work. He had said they were all sick. Everyone in the synagogue was shot. This doctor had been involved in other killings, too. He had arrived at Buchenwald with his children, and the underground leadership said: "The children will grow up without him because he is a murderer and he should not come out alive."

However, the prisoners were in need of medical care. This doctor's life was spared so he could help others. "Always, we made decisions in the protection unit to protect the camp, protect people, protect the innocent," Gustav said.

By the end of the tribunal, when the clock in the foyer had struck midnight, all the tension in the room had been deflated along with the midday breeze. I once asked Papa, who didn't have an answer, why it would be windy during the day but when night fell, everything was calm. Calm was us now. No one wanted to seek vengeance against Gustav after all. The Intellectuals simply asked him to leave Écouis. They didn't want to see him and be reminded of the camps.

This spoke to a larger divide among us boys, I think. There were those of us who wanted our memories of those prison walls because freedom brought with it, at least for me, a feeling of falling and insecurity. I was supposed to feel safe now, but living on the edge of a razor blade, I had gotten used to how to position myself so I wouldn't fall. This new life, which the Intellectuals had embraced somehow, frightened me more than the camps did. The horrors of the camps had become known to me. The unknown felt like an abyss I couldn't climb out of.

As a parade of the Polish boys walked Gustav to the train station the next morning, I hung back, like I usually did, pondering why I felt so terribly alone, so terribly afraid, when my nightmare was over and I was surrounded by hundreds of boys just like me. I had traveled through the valley of death and made it out the other side. It was like there was something buried in those depths that I needed to find, some treasure, before I could move into the light.

Buchenwald Boys headed to Palestine doing the hora the night
before leaving Écouis.

9

"Yea, though I walk through the valley of the shadow of death, I will fear no evil, for Thou art with me; Thy rod and Thy staff, they comfort me."

—Psalm 23:4

A FURNITURE TRUCK, larger than any truck I had ever seen, crept along the driveway, stopping not far from the front doors.

About a hundred of us boys stood outside, gaping and watching. I could see that some of the boys were in awe, like me, at the size of the vehicle. Those of us from the smaller towns found so much of France new, like those bathtubs and bathrooms the size of the homes.

When the truck stopped, a couple of the older boys swung open the cargo-bed doors and leaped inside.

As the older boys moved about, I spied shirts and jackets swaying on hangers hung on clothing racks. There were also large boxes, piled to the ceiling, that the older boys opened and then sorted.

After about an hour, the older boys stepped off the truck and announced that the clothes had been separated into sizes. We should figure out what size we each were and then, in small groups of four, come into the truck and choose an assortment of new garments, including underwear, socks, and a pair of shoes.

The boys near the front started to jostle one another to see who would go first. While the boys argued, I slyly moved in between them, inching my way forward, until I was in the second group.

After I got my clothes, I bounded up the stairs of the main building, two steps at a time, until I reached one of those bathrooms.

I locked the door, then slowly took off the Nazi Youth uniform.

I gestured to start the bath and then stopped, realizing I didn't know how to turn it on. In Poland, Mama would wash me in a big tin washbasin with water she'd heated on the stove and which she had fetched from a well. We didn't have what Salek said were hot-water tanks or faucets or piping for running water inside a house.

I picked up a pair of dark-gray wool shorts and slowly slipped them on, followed by a short-sleeved cotton button-down shirt. I then combed my hair with my fingers and spit.

Finally, ever so carefully, afraid of what I would see, I looked at myself in the mirror.

I jumped and turned quickly, thinking there was someone else in the room with me.

When I realized that the reflection looking back was me, I stared into my face.

I was old, just like Lulek had told Rabbi Shachter. I was no longer a child with puffy cheeks and soft, downy hair. My eyes had creases in the corners, and there were dark-brown patches on my face from where I had been scalded with the burning can of meat. My hair was shorn. I was bald in a few places, either from malnutrition or from having my head shaved by the Nazis so many times that I lost count. The Nazis said shaving our hair was to stop us from getting lice. But Jakow told Abe and me that our hair was actually used in the Nazi bombs and to stuff pillows. Ilse Koch, the wife of the Nazi *kommandant* of Buchenwald, used prisoners' hair, skin, teeth, and bones to make lamps and lampshades, even art that she hung in her home. Jakow said prisoners called her a witch.

I ran my fingers down my cheeks. The last time I'd looked at myself in a mirror was in the ghetto. Mama had trimmed my hair with Papa's tailoring scissors she had managed to take from his shop before the Nazis shut it down. She had held up a cracked mirror for me to admire her work. That was the last time I knew what I looked like.

I was ten.

As I searched my face, its lines and folds that weren't there before, and then my eyes, I didn't recognize myself. I didn't see Mama or Papa, Chaim, Motel, Moishe, Abram, or Leah.

I couldn't remember what they looked like, but I knew enough to know I didn't resemble them.

I was a stranger even to myself.

———

A month had passed. Quarantine was over, not that many of us were following it anyway.

Salek, Abe, Joe, Marek, and I asked the OSE worker everyone called Nini for money for photographs. A lot of the boys had crushes on Nini. Nini had even wilder black hair than Madame Minc and large, dreamy eyes. Salek told Nini that Ralph would hand the photos out in Germany at the refugee camps to see if anyone could recognize us.

Nini eyed us suspiciously. At the mention of Ralph's name, I thought she flinched, as if she didn't like him very much. Nonetheless, she opened a tin and handed us each some French francs. As we turned to leave, she told us to wait. On a piece of OSE stationary, she wrote a note in French, which she handed to Salek. "The photographer doesn't speak Yiddish. I know him. Give him this to tell him what you want."

We found our stolen bikes and rode quickly into town, my heart pounding, my thoughts racing. I wanted to ask Ralph if I could go with him to Germany and then maybe to Russia to find Chaim. I wanted to get the photographs taken quickly so that I didn't miss Ralph before he left.

When we reached a fountain near the center of town, we hopped off the bikes, leaving them on the ground, not propped up against walls like the French did. We then used Ralph's map to find our way to the photography shop.

We spent the entire morning sitting on stools as the photographer snapped our mug shots. We then had to wait a few hours for the photos to be developed.

We meandered back to the fountain, dipping our hands and feet in the cool, gurgling water, which was refreshing on such a hot day. France, I had discovered, was more humid, the sun more scorching, than even the hottest afternoons of July back in Poland.

I looked around. It was a few days after France had celebrated the July 14 holiday marking the storming of the Bastille, which started the French Revolution. Madame Minc, not Salek, had explained to us that the French Revolution had resulted in the overthrow of the monarchy and led to the will of the people and democracy. We boys were given sugary pastries and croissants for breakfast and macaroons frosted in the colors of the French flag—red, white, and blue—for dessert at dinner. After that, some singers from Paris performed revolutionary songs. Perhaps inspired by the singing, some of the boys stood up and sang folk songs by Jewish artists, including Mordechai Gebirtig, that they said they had learned at Buchenwald.

I looked around at the village of Écouis and the large Christian church that seemed to be its center point. It looked like the village had celebrated, too, as there were red, white, and blue ribbons draped from open windows and balconies, and from the sides of buildings French flags flopped in the weak breeze. For a moment, I imagined what the town might have looked like under German occupation. Like Skarżysko-Kamienna, Nazi red flags and banners would have been hoisted.

When we returned to the photography shop to pick up our prints, Ralph was there speaking to the photographer in French. When the photographer handed me mine, I stared, like I had in the mirror, at my face. Before leaving Buchenwald, all of us, including me, had to do an interview with a

Buchenwald Boys having their picture taken. Romek, far right, second row; Abe, front row center.

representative from the American Army. In the interview, I was asked why I was at the camp. I had replied because I was Jewish. I was then asked my name. I tilted my head to the side and stared at the man, my mind searching for who I was. I finally spat out my number, 117098, which I had first been given when I went to work at HASAG. The boys who had been in Auschwitz had their numbers tattooed onto their skin. My number, I was just forced to memorize, and it was on my identity papers. In some of the camps, my number was also on the badge I had to wear along with the yellow star indicating I was Jewish.

"117098," I told the interviewer several times. Finally, after much prompting by Rabbi Marcus, who was translating for the interviewer, I said my Hebrew name, Rachmil. I had forgotten I was Romek, which was my Polish name.

As we left the photography shop, I asked Ralph if it was hard to learn French. "Not really. I'm a quick learner," he replied with a smug look. "Besides, for Communists, language is irrelevant," he continued in Yiddish. "Language is just something else that divides people, like religion. There are lots of Communists in Paris," he then added in Polish. "They meet at certain clubs and bistros. I can take you sometime if you like. They taught me a bit of French before telling me not to learn anything more because one day there will be just one language, making us all equal."

––––––

When we got back to the sanatorium, Elie and the other boys who wanted to re-embrace our religion had prepared the table for Shabbat with Kiddush wine, which is a sweet wine; matzo; candles; matches; and challah. Before Shabbat, the Intellectuals wanted to do a Kaddish for the dead. About a quarter of the boys were leaving the next day by bus for Marseille, where they would board the ship to take them to Palestine.

A crowd of boys had formed around the Intellectuals and was pushing in close. From what I could see, the non-Intellectuals were not happy about the Shabbat.

I remained in the hallway. As I watched, I remembered the last Shabbat I had with my family in our home in Poland. There were rumors that the Nazis were creating a Jewish Quarter and would move all of us Jews there. That Shabbat was sad, because my brothers and sister knew there were problems ahead, but Papa forced smiles and kept repeating we would be all right. I could tell my siblings didn't trust the words of Papa, and I felt heartbroken because until that moment, he was infallible, our rock we all leaned on. It was on that night I saw that even Mama and Papa had lying eyes. Nothing they said could take away the cold shiver running through my blood. Mama and Papa wanted this Shabbat to be special, they said, and normal, despite the streets outside drenched with Jewish blood. Papa said the Kiddush prayer, blessed the wine, blessed the bread, and all the while, I could see the strain on his face. "I believe in humanity," he finally said. On that night, Chaim didn't play the violin after, like he usually did at our Friday dinners.

I peered into the dining hall. Some of the boys circling the Intellectuals were cursing under their breath. A few started muttering that there was no God.

I heard one of the Intellectuals announce that the Kaddish was for the millions of Jews who the media were reporting dead. "No, no, no . . . ," I started to murmur. During Shabbat, Mama and Papa and the other elders would often recite the Kaddish for those who had died. But they wanted to do Kaddish for so many. I wanted, I needed to believe more of us were still alive.

Walking slowly backward, I bumped into another boy, who hissed at me to watch where I was going. I quickly spun around and ran out of the building, skirting past some of the boys headed to Palestine who were outside. They had linked arms and were doing the hora. Their faces were alight. They were happy.

Breathless, I ran, murmuring that I had to find Papa. I wasn't interested in Palestine, just finding my family.

I had to get to Leah and find out what she knew about Papa, Chaim, Nathan . . . Golda and Moishe and Motel.

I rounded a pine tree and heard Ralph calling my name.

I stopped quickly, stumbling over my feet but managing to stay upright.

Bent over at the waist, huffing and puffing, I walked toward Ralph. He was sitting, smoking, under the willow tree.

In between gasping for breath, I managed to get out that I couldn't wait for the OSE to get me an ID or a train ticket. I needed to see my sister in Feldafing. "Can you help?"

"Do you have any money?" Ralph asked coolly, like he already knew the answer, butting out his cigarette on the bark of the tree.

"I don't have money," I said, finally catching my breath.

Ralph sighed. "Do you even know how to get to Feldafing?"

I shook my head.

He laughed. "I can take you to the train station if you like, show you how to get to Feldafing if the trains are running." Ralph was one of those people, I was catching on quickly enough, who liked being needed. I saw these people at the camps; being needed was what kept some people alive.

I huffed out a thank-you.

As we walked, Ralph explained that I had to take the train from Écouis to Paris, then transfer to a train to Munich. When we got to the train station, we learned that the next train for Paris was in an hour. We sat on a bench overlooking the tree where I had vomited when I arrived at Écouis as Ralph had me recite from memory the directions to Feldafing over and over again so I wouldn't forget. After, he dug into a black army duffel bag resting beside him. From it, he withdrew a uniform. "This is a sous-lieutenant outfit of the French military," he explained, passing me the uniform piece by piece. The trousers and jacket were brown and came with a thick leather belt and a cotton hat. There were ribbons sewn onto the lapel, indicating the rank of the soldier who had worn it last.

I shrugged, holding the jacket out in front of me. "What's this for?"

"You wear the uniform and you can get on the train for free."

I scoffed. "Who would believe I was a French soldier?"

"Trust me. You'll pass."

"Everyone will know I am wearing some dead man's uniform," I protested. "And I've worn the clothes of dead people for far too long."

Ralph laughed. "The man who owned this uniform is not dead," he said. "And you'll be safe in it."

"Thanks," I said uncertainly, tucking the uniform under my arm.

Ralph eyed me up and down. "Here, take my backpack, too," he said, dumping the remaining items from the knapsack on the ground. I saw various pieces of French Army uniforms, berets, and books, one of which I recognized. "I thought you didn't believe in religion," I said to him, pointing at the mahzor, a Jewish prayer book used on high

100

holidays—Rosh Hashana, our New Year, and Yom Kippur, which follows Rosh Hashana. During Yom Kippur, Mama told me, Jews pray for atonement from God for their sins.

"Carry the bag over your shoulder. Makes you look like a soldier returning from war," he said, ignoring my question.

"But . . . ," I started, then stopped. I swallowed hard. "Ralph," I began slowly, uncertain whether I could trust him not to go to Madame Minc or Nini, who I was sure, along with the professor, would bar me from leaving if they knew my true intentions. "I don't plan on coming back. I'm going to Russia from Feldafing. I'm never leaving my sister again. I might not be able to return your things."

Ralph studied me hard, like he was trying to read my thoughts, making me feel uncomfortable. He then cocked a smile and nodded. "Joining the Communist movement!" he said. It wasn't a question.

"Something like that," I said with a shrug.

"I'll find you in Feldafing," I caught Ralph saying as I tossed my French Army uniform into the duffel bag, then stood up, saying I needed to find a washroom to change.

"Écouis to Paris train station east, then on to Germany, first Munich and then Starnberg, which is just a little southwest," I recited.

———

I didn't need the uniform or any identification at all.

Many of the passengers on the trains were Jews, some even children younger than I was and traveling alone.

When the ticket taker came, I started to speak with him in first Polish and then Yiddish, pointing at my uniform. He shrugged and smiled, knowing the uniform wasn't mine. A survivor who spoke French translated for me that I was going to find my sister, who was in a displaced-persons camp in Germany.

"*Dieu soit avec toi, mon fils,*" the ticket taker said, handing me a piece of paper.

I shook my head, indicating I didn't understand him.

"He says, 'May God be with you, my son,'" the translator, an older woman, said. "The ticket he has given you," the woman added, taking the piece of paper and studying it, "takes you all the way to Feldafing and back."

I looked up at the ticket taker and thanked him.

On the stretch of train from Paris to Germany, French train staff handed out cheese, bread, tomatoes, peaches, and milk. I wasn't hungry, so I gave my portion to the woman. She was traveling with a very small child. She told me, when the little girl was asleep, that the child was her sister's grandchild. The entire family except for her and the child were still missing, presumed dead.

———

When the train entered Germany, panic gripped me.

The sky was much the same as in France, the grasses, too, elephant long and blowing in the breeze. But it still felt like a steel curtain separated the two countries, and I was on the wrong side. I remembered, then, the Germany I saw when I was transported from Skarżysko-Kamienna to various camps, eventually Częstochowa, then Buchenwald. The stations where we stopped were noisy, full of barking Alsatian dogs and Nazi men shooting their weapons in the air.

102

Orders, always orders being shouted. Sometimes I would hear the sizzle of a hose, knowing then that someone was spraying the cattle compartments with water. I'd tilt my head up, stick my tongue out, and lick whatever droplets dripped through the holes in the wood. That was often my only water for the day.

Now Germany was silent.

As the train moved inland, the landscape darkened, in part because of the thickening forests, in part also because of the burned-out army tanks and the relics of villages we passed, some with houses that were now just stone frames.

"What have I done?" I whispered. "I have made a mistake coming back here." Life breathed in France, even if I was not part of it. Here, Germany, was the charred remains, like the corpses piled in the camps.

I was reminded suddenly of something Mama used to say: "We fear that which we want most." I wanted to go home, even if home was no longer a place but just meant I was with my family.

My dreams, I realized with a thud, were easier when they remained unsung.

———

I was on the train for two days with no money, but the men and women manning the food carts gave out free food to Jewish children, including me: bread and butter, sometimes a tomato sandwich and an apple.

By the time I made it to Feldafing, night was falling.

The camp grew up and around me, like a town that starts thin and then grows heavy. Alongside redbrick buildings were cylinder tents and people milling about. Most stared as I walked past, stared with haggard, sad eyes. An old, bald man with a misshapen hand and bowed legs from rickets directed me to a building that he said was an office.

The staff members were busy, pushing papers about, talking on telephones, and typing. I stood in the doorway unnoticed until I called out. A woman approached, tinier than even me, with a mole beside her mouth that twitched when she spoke. She said in Yiddish that there were so many people in the camp, thousands, and every day there were new arrivals. The office couldn't keep up documenting all the people, including listing where everyone lived. Jewish survivors of the death camps slept wherever they could find beds until more tents arrived. Many slept three or four to a cot, like when we were in the barracks, but at least here they had clean blankets and fresh water. Food, while not a lot, was being shipped in by various aid organizations. The woman said that if I headed right when I left the office and walked for about ten minutes straight down the main road, I'd find an old pantyhose factory where many young Polish women had grouped together. If my sister wasn't there, likely someone in the building would know where she was.

I walked slowly, the surroundings settling in around me, the cooking fires, the sunken faces I passed, the heaviness of the camp. I felt I was in a movie, moving through a ghost town, the specters being those of us who survived.

Finally, I saw the long building the woman in the office had said was a pantyhose factory. It was shaped like a rectangular box, like the HASAG munitions factory, and that sent another cold shiver through me.

I slid open the steel front door.

It was dark inside, lit by only a few candles and kerosene lamps.

"I'm looking for Leah," I called out. My voice echoed against the cement walls of the foyer.

I turned a corner. Several women, seeing me, stopped what they were doing and approached. They touched me, running their hands up and down my body, calling out that there was now a man in the building.

I pushed my way through them, staring at each face, looking for Leah's.

I wove my way through the long building, through clotheslines stretched from wall to wall airing blankets and dresses. There were mattresses set on the floor and wooden dressers being used as room dividers.

Finally, I reached the end of the building. There was only one group of women left to ask if one of them was Leah. They were sitting and lying on a large mattress. As I neared them, they stared, unlike the other women in the building, their eyes wide and curious.

One nudged a woman lying on her stomach. She rolled over, and when her eyes fell on me, she sat bolt upright.

I recognized her immediately. Leah. My Leah.

Her face was broad and, despite her thinness, her frame was solid like I remembered Papa's. Her nose was familiar, like if I could recall Chaim's and Moishe's faces, hers would be the same.

Shaking, she stood and walked toward me slowly and carefully, like she was walking a tightrope at the traveling circuses that would come to Skarżysko-Kamienna.

"Romek," she whispered in a hoarse voice. "Romek. I thought you had been killed . . ."

I recognized that voice, too, her voice, the voice that would sing me Yiddish folk songs and tell me stories.

I stared into Leah's eyes. I recognized those, too: they were just like Mama's eyes.

10

LEAH, THE OTHER women from her room, and I sat by a blazing outside fire, cuddled in rough wool blankets, talking quietly, staring at the stars, which were bright. Leah sat behind me, her long legs stretched around me as she stroked my back, rubbed my hands, and massaged my shoulders.

As the night temperature dipped, the other women went inside. Just Leah and I remained. She rocked me like she had when I was young, singing Yiddish songs, so close that I could feel her moist breath on the skin of my ear. She was treating me like a baby, but I didn't mind.

I fell asleep in her arms to *"Oyfn Pripetchik,"* her voice having deepened in the years we'd been apart—so much so, I was unsure where she began and Mama left off.

> *A fire burns on the hearth*
> *And it is warm in the little house.*
> *And the rabbi is teaching little children*
> *The alphabet . . .*

"I don't know where anyone is," Leah told me in the morning as we ate leftover cholent. Her voice was hoarse now, maybe because we'd both fallen asleep outside, under the chuppah of the Milky Way, and Germany, unlike France, held damp, cool dawns.

"I thought you were with Mama and Golda," I said in a choked voice. I didn't want this conversation. I didn't want to know. My hands moved to cover my ears the way I would do in the ghetto, when I didn't want to hear the screams; the cries; the mamas whimpering; the papas arguing over the lack of złoty, the absence of bread, the long lines for rations; the sons protesting that we should have left Poland when we had the chance.

"Do you remember selection? When the Jewish Quarter was liquidated? When the Nazis picked us to go in one line or another?" she asked.

I didn't. I wasn't there, I reminded her. I had already gone to work at the munitions factory. Chaim had gotten me the job, then had returned to the barn where he had told Nathan and me to hide. He took Nathan away first. I sat for another full day and night in the barn alone, listening to the night owls and the sighs of cows. When Chaim did come back for me, he took me to the ghetto to say goodbye to Mama, and then he brought me to HASAG.

Leah stared off into nothing and started nodding like she remembered, remembered I wasn't there and that neither were Papa or Abram, who had been sent to work at HASAG a few months before I was.

"An SS officer asked Golda if she wanted to go with Mama or with me," Leah eventually picked up. "Mama and I were in two different lines. I was going to work at the women's quarters at HASAG. I was there all along, not far from you but far enough away that we never met."

Leah then pushed her eyes tightly shut, as if she were trying to block out the images in front of her. "Mama, though, she was in line with very young children and the old and sick. Mama was alone. Golda refused to leave her," she continued in a strained voice. "Golda went with Mama, and they were put on a train."

Watching Leah, her pinched face, her bottom lip that trembled, I could tell there was more.

"I met someone who knew about those trains," Leah finally pressed on. "Here in Feldafing." Her voice was cradled sadness.

I closed my eyes, too.

"This person told me Golda and Mama were taken to Treblinka," Leah pressed on. "Treblinka," she repeated. "No supplies went there. The trains that went to Treblinka were full of people. When they returned, they were always empty. Romek, it was a death camp."

I knew from Jakow at Buchenwald about Treblinka. It was near Bug River, where during summer holidays Papa and Mama would take us. But at Treblinka, Jakow had said, Jews would go into the bathhouses expecting water to rain down on them from the showers. Instead, gas would leak out, killing everyone inside. Then the Nazis would take the bodies to crematoriums to burn. The sky would fill with what looked like flakes of snow but were actually the charred remains of Jews.

"But where is Nathan, then?" I mumbled. "And the others?"

"Nathan wasn't with Golda or Mama," Leah said, shaking her head. "I think Chaim left him with a farmer."

I remembered then, hiding in the barn under the hay, trying to keep Nathan quiet by feeding him candies. He didn't understand the importance of silence, not the way I did. He was just a toddler and wanted to play, to giggle, to cry. He wasn't like the other toddlers who lived in our apartment building in the ghetto, who somehow knew what was going on and were little adults in tiny bodies, always somber, like their voices had left.

I shuddered then, remembering when, just before the ghetto was formed, Papa had sent me to live with a farming family. The Brankowskis. If Nathan, who was outgoing, talkative, inquisitive, but also stubborn, had been sent to a farm, he would never have made it.

———

A few days after our last Shabbat in our home, Chaim drove me to live with the Brankowskis.

Papa, Chaim told me, had used the remaining złoty in the family bank account to pay Mr. Brankowski to take me in. "You will be safe there," he had said as we drove. "They have dark hair like us. Imagine our good fortune to find a Polish family who is dark."

I didn't understand, at first, what Chaim meant when he said this. But I soon did. I was to be passed off as one of the Brankowski children's cousins.

At the Brankowskis' farm, that's when I first felt that sense of falling.

I'd wake in the night, startled, unsure of where I was, like

I had been transported somewhere I wasn't meant to be. A hollow, cool, and dark place, like the outcropping of rocks on the Kamienna River where I'd hide during games of seek-and-find—hide along with the worms that burrow in the mud of the embankment and the snails.

At first, the feeling would leave by breakfast, a meal of porridge and milk. But as the stares of the three Brankowski children bore into me, their silences, broken by their whispers and giggles, I found myself slipping for longer and longer periods of time.

Every morning and every evening, Mrs. Brankowski and her eldest daughter would teach me the stations of the Catholic cross and make sure I knew the Lord's Prayer. They would remind me to never use my Yiddish name, Rachmil. I was Romek. "Whatever you do, never say or let on that you are Jewish," Mr. and Mrs. Brankowski would tell me. "Never speak Yiddish. In fact, forget every word of Yiddish you've ever learned. From now on, you communicate only in Polish."

One night, I overheard Mrs. Brankowski tell her husband that I had "good looks." That meant I could pass for a Polish Christian. I didn't look Jewish. Another night, I overheard her discussing with Mr. Brankowski how Papa hadn't given them enough money for food, let alone a new Kennkarte, or identity card, which every Pole had to carry. The new card, she said, would say I was Christian, not Jewish, and a nephew of theirs from Warsaw.

I didn't go to school. I was sent out to work in the field every morning looking after the Brankowskis' cows. I had been a town boy, the son of a haberdasher. I didn't know *animals. The closest I'd been to any were the horses that drew our neighbors' carts that helped them plough their fields. Papa would borrow them in the summer to take us to the cabin for our vacation.*

On those barren fields that turned slushy in the first snows, those cows would head east, when Mr. Brankowski told me to walk them following the sun.

Every day, the bones of my legs ached from all the walking, my arms and hands numb from milking. My belly groaned and started to stick out from lack of food, for my meals became mostly bland porridge and the Brankowskis' leftovers, including the bones of meat that I sucked in the tiny storage room where I slept. The room was the farthest away from the fire and the coal stove. It was always cold, but not as cold as the barracks at the camps.

My only company on the farm was a tiny redwing that would perch itself on the ledge outside the window in the storage room. Golda told me once that nature brings us messages. "Open your heart, close your eyes, and you will see the magic around you," she would say as we walked to the Jewish bakery where Mama would buy unleavened bread, challah, rugelach—which are tasty pastries—and onion rolls. Once with Golda, we saw a deer. She said it was a positive sign that she would have a child. She rubbed her abdomen and murmured a prayer. A week later, she learned she was pregnant with Nathan. Another time, we saw a string of frogs hopping from the far side of the path back toward a stream. "New beginnings," Golda had said then with a wide smile.

The redwing would sing me its pretty song. And that

ravine inside me grew even wider as I was reminded of Mama, who was not with me.

One day, not long after the Brankowski family celebrated Christmas, when the ice of winter had not yet frozen the lakes and rivers, I just left. For an entire day, I drifted like the swells of snowbanks until I found the Kamienna River. I followed the river until I reached the town and could go no farther, unless I swam across.

Before the ghetto but after the Germans came, Abram and I found ourselves out, walking the streets, cornered by Jewish police. The Germans had imposed a curfew, meaning Jews could not leave their homes past a certain time at night. Three guards ran toward us, trying to catch us. We ran, behind buildings, down alleyways, until we reached the river. We heard the whistles closing in on us.

"Swim," Abram hissed at me as he jumped into the river. I didn't know how. "Just splash your arms like the way dogs paddle," he called out.

Like on that night, I leaped into the river, with its rapids, and waved my arms so hard, so wild, until I made it to the other side. I dragged myself up on the opposite bank, soaking wet. Shivering from the cold, my teeth chattering and my toes frozen, I was sure I had frostbite. I meandered until I found someone who told me where our apartment was in the ghetto.

When Papa saw me, his eyes turned red. He came at me like Mama's steaming kettles for tea. For the first time in my life, he picked me up in those strong arms of his, laid me across his lap, and spanked me until my screams dimmed to whimpers. It took nearly a week before I could sit and it no longer hurt.

That was the start of Papa turning on me, when I believed he no longer loved me.

———

"When the ghetto was formed, many of the Polish farmers who had taken in Jewish children were forced to turn them in to the Nazis," Leah was saying. "The farmers were given sugar and flour as rewards. If a farmer didn't hand over a Jewish child, they and their families would be killed. Neighbors informed on neighbors about children who had just appeared. There weren't enough Nazis in Poland to oversee the Jews in the ghettos, so the Polish farmers did their work for them. They were forced to, Romek. If Nathan were on a farm, if that is where Chaim had taken him, I don't think he would have survived," she said.

"But there were farmers who defied the Nazis," I quickly added. "Jakow said that in Poland, there was an underground network of people hiding Jewish children." I told Leah then what Jakow had told me: of rumors that had made it to Buchenwald of hundreds, if not thousands of Jewish men, women, and children being hidden by Poles, including in the animals' cages at the Warsaw Zoo. The brickmasons told us boys that children were even being smuggled out of the Warsaw Ghetto and placed with Polish families and in orphanages.

"It's possible," Leah said slowly. "But if Nathan is alive, we face another hurdle. Nathan won't know who he is. He was three in the fall of 1942. For the past three years, he would have believed, would have been told to tell people, he was a Christian child. If he is alive, he may have even been

114

baptized a Christian and believe now he is the child of the family who took him in. The family, even now, might not tell him his true identity, thinking all of us are dead. He's their child now."

"When we find Chaim, he'll know where he took Nathan. Then we can all go together and get him. We'll tell him who he is."

Leah closed her eyes.

Dread moved through me.

"Where is Chaim?" I asked slowly. "He's in Russia, right? Because he was in the military, he went with other Polish soldiers to train and fight, right?"

"He was shot," she whispered.

Falling. I was falling again.

"He was sent to Treblinka, too, but on another transport than Golda and Mama. He was a soldier, Romek," Leah said. "Chaim was never safe staying in Poland. The Nazis were killing all the Polish soldiers—anyone who could rise up and defeat them. We should have forced Chaim to leave as soon as the Nazis came. But he wouldn't abandon his family."

I closed my eyes. When I was ill in Écouis, when for nearly a week I could barely get out of bed, the professor had talked to me about the French painter Jean-Léon Gérôme. The artist had done two pieces of related works, one of which was called *Truth Coming Out of Her Well*. The professor had said that the meaning of the paintings was that truth has been deceived. "Falsehoods, lies, ambitions of men, greed have kept truth hidden in the bottom of a well," he had said.

The liars and the actors had won.

Truth lost, I thought.

My dream of us all being together was being torn apart.
I had nothing left to hang on to.

———

"What next?" I asked Leah.

We were walking arm in arm. I'd been in Feldafing for nearly a week. When we weren't talking about family, Leah rekindling in me memories I had forgotten, we went to the theater at the camp and watched movies, silent black-and-white films. By blazing fires at night we would listen to story-tellers and to music, often played by musicians who had survived the death camps through being part of symphonies that would perform for the Nazis. Or we would walk, just walk.

"I want you to meet someone," she said. "I've met someone, Romek. His name is Abram, like our Abram."

I could tell by the way Leah's Abram looked at her, how his hand brushed up against her skin, how his speech became soft when he spoke to her and me, that he was in love with her, the way Chaim was in love with Golda and Papa was with Mama.

He asked me if I knew anything about the stars, astronomy, the study of the skies, because he said he did. I huffed that I didn't know much.

Abram was not tall, like my family. But he had our jet-black hair. He had a square jaw. He was from Łódź and, like Chaim, had been in the Polish Army. But he had made it to Russia. He had returned to Poland with the Soviet Union's Red Army, where he'd met Leah.

He asked if I had seen *The Great Dictator*, starring the

English actor Charlie Chaplin. They didn't have it in the camp, not yet, but he wanted to see it. I said no. I hadn't been to the theater in France.

That Friday in Feldafing, Abram held Shabbat. I sat on one side of Leah, Abram on the other.

As a rabbi at the camp did the prayers, Abram leaned across Leah and whispered to me that he'd heard *The Great Dictator* was one of the best films ever made. Maybe we could all watch it together in Paris.

I tucked my hands underneath my legs, as I felt them rise toward my ears to cover them. I didn't want to hear Abram speaking, not anymore. Leah was trying, trying to include me in her life, to bring me back to the living. I didn't want to disappoint her. But I also wanted her all to myself. I didn't want to go back to France. I wanted to stay with her.

"In *The Great Dictator*, this actor, Charlie Chaplin, dresses like Adolf Hitler," Leah added with a smile. "We all talk about it in the camp."

I balled my fists. For the first time since I left Écouis, I wanted to fight, to punch, to hurt something.

I whispered to Leah that I needed fresh air.

I would be outside.

―――――

"We're moving to Palestine," Leah said as we meandered back to the pantyhose factory, my legs loping, slogging. I had little to no energy left inside me, no fuel. I wanted to melt into the ground, become a part of the earth. My only living relative, the one part of a dream that was real, that I could touch, was telling me she and Abram were getting married and moving to Palestine. "We were supposed to stay together," I wanted to shout at her, "and find the others."

On the other side of Leah was Abram. She had slipped her arm through Abram's or he through hers.

Golda once said that when lovers walked, their steps synchronized, like they became one.

As my eyes blurred, Leah and Abram looked like one person. I felt bile move up the back of my throat.

"I heard from Madame Minc," Leah said. "She sent a telegraph to the office. She wants you to return to France, and I think it would be best, too."

Startled, I stopped. "Y-you mean, I'm not coming with you?" I stammered.

Leah swallowed hard. "The OSE has moved to Château de Ferrières for the summer. Madame Minc has sent directions for me to give to you."

"I can move to Palestine with you!" I said. I stomped my foot and crossed my arms across my chest.

"It will be hard in Palestine," she said in a soft voice, stroking my shoulder. "Abram and I will be working on a farm. There are no businesses there. We just don't know what to expect. Abram and I need to establish our lives and then bring you after that. In France, with the OSE, you can go to school, get healthy again, be a part of something, be safe, and have food and friends. Remember how you used to love pulling and twisting wires together, watching Moishe build his radios? Study engineering. Then we can all be together."

I started to shake my head.

"It's what Mama would want," Leah cut in. "Romek, remember when Papa would talk about the story of our prophets?"

I shook my head and covered my ears. I didn't remember or didn't want to remember.

"In the darkest of times, our heroes always had aids who came to their sides," Leah said. "All the prophets had something, someone guiding them. Follow your path, and these people will appear and will lead you where you are supposed to go. Be open to the people along the way directing you. They will lead you home, the home inside your heart. I am one of them, and when you're through your darkness, which the OSE is the best equipped to help you with, I will find you, and we will be together. I promise. Do you trust me, Romek?"

I bit the side of my mouth. I didn't believe her. I didn't believe anybody.

Leah took my hands and placed them on my heart. I could feel my pulse.

"With every step, I know you will want to turn away," she said, standing real close and speaking softly into my ear. "But be strong. Go forward. Place one foot in front of you and then another, until love becomes your guide again. Follow it, the scent of it, the whiff of a perfume that reminds you of home, a fragrance that takes you somewhere you have never been before. And one by one, people will appear, places will come into view that were just whispers. These are your torches, lighting your way."

11

AT HASAG, SUNDAY was the day Abram and I could spend time with Papa.

But still, on Sundays, despite it being a holiday, the SS men would come, ordering us to line up in rows on the HASAG Appellplatz. The SS would move in real close, sometimes ordering a Jew to open his mouth so they could study the teeth and gums and see if the person was healthy. The SS would move in and around us like snakes with their pants tucked into their tall black boots, looking for those with the slumping backs or the shakes from fever or other illnesses. With a nod of the head or a flick of an arm, the SS officers would direct some to the left, others to the right. One way meant life. The other death. Replacements from another ghetto were on their way anyway.

On this one Sunday, Papa and Abram were ordered to go to the left, while I was sent to the right.

I scanned the men standing with me: bent over, coughing, wheezing, some yellow from working with picric acid. I was on the wrong side.

Without thinking, I rushed toward an SS man, who hadn't seen to which line I had been sent. I waved wildly at Papa's line, shaking my head, saying "no, no, no" in German.

He stared at me, the mustache above his lip twitching like he was about to laugh.

I raised my hands up in front of me like in Christian prayer and then pointed to the line of the sick. "Yes, yes, yes," I then said in German.

The SS man's eyes lit up.

I then pointed again at Papa, whose eyes were wide, the whites like lamps on a moonless night. I was pretending I didn't want to go to Papa's line. I wanted to go to the other line.

The SS man finally pursed his lips and slapped my head, ordering me to go to the left.

I took a gamble that the SS man would send me where I didn't want to go. My ruse worked.

I lived another day, then.

———

On the train back to France, I nestled myself in a corner seat by the window, pulling my torso in tight and away from the two Jewish families who shared the cab with me. I didn't want to speak to anyone.

For most of the journey, I pretended to be asleep, my eyes shut tight, but the truth was that I couldn't sleep. My mind tossed and turned, thinking of Leah, Treblinka, Chaim and Nathan, HASAG, Abram . . . how many times I was so close to death but I lived, me, the baby of the family, the one with the least odds of making it. I had. Why?

I listened to the conversations around me. The sounds of

the stations when we stopped to pick up and drop off passengers—heeled shoes walking on cement, the giggles of children, the train's whistle, the chugging of its coupling rods that made the wheels turn.

The closer the train drew to Paris, the more anxious I became, wanting to get off and just go somewhere different, to disappear.

As the train slowed coming into a station, I began collecting my few belongings to disembark. But as I stood to leave, my eyes locked with those of a girl sitting across from me. She was about my age and just staring. She had golden-red hair and blue eyes that looked green when our compartment lit up as the train went under a lamppost. Her nose was dotted with freckles. In the world that seemed dank and gray, I thought for a moment, she was starlight, and I found myself slipping back down into my seat.

She was holding the hand of an older man sitting beside her. They were gripping each other tight, like they feared letting go.

I remembered then the night Chaim had taken me to HASAG. I held Mama tight around the waist, begging to not leave her. "Don't worry. We will see each other soon. Go with your brother Chaim. He got you a job," she cooed.

I sat back down in my seat. The girl gave me a weak smile and a nod before settling back against the arm of the man.

I knew this girl.

I couldn't say from where.

Maybe just a dream. But something about her made me decide to go on to Château de Ferrières.

Leah's Abram told me before I left Feldafing that the Rothschild family who owned Château de Ferrières was one of the wealthiest families in all of Europe. They came by their fortune through banking. The Château de Ferrières was built in the 1850s, and during the Nazi occupation of France, the château was taken over by the Germans, who looted it of its prized art, statues, and furniture.

If I had thought the home in Écouis was the largest I'd ever seen, the château was a French Masada, large, grand, a castle with manicured lawns, tailored trees, bursting rosebushes, and statues. The windows of the castle itself twinkled from the lights inside, like gold with jewels. To me, walking onto the property was like walking into the story Jakow would tell about the lost princess who was eventually found in a palace made of gold, surrounded by a fortress made of pearls.

I wished Jakow could see the Château de Ferrières, I thought. This was the castle he was talking about in his story.

I dropped my army bag on the cement steps leading up to the entrance to the Château de Ferrières.

I twirled around, my arms outstretched, wide and welcoming, intoxicated from the perfumed aromas of the flower beds, realizing that for years, the scents around me were decaying bodies, our own excrement, the filth of diseases, and body odor. Then I stopped and stared down at the long gardens. Even when Jakow told the story of the princess and the palace, being a poor boy from Skarżysko-Kamienna, I never imagined in my mind a kingdom like this.

I stayed very still, listening to the gurgles and tumbles of water from the many fountains. Then I heard voices carried on a soft summer breeze. Boys' voices, rising, but they were not coming from inside the palace. I picked up the backpack and followed the voices, around one of the corner towers of the massive complex, until I spied a one-story, long, bunker-like building and gasped.

It looked like another barracks.

The front door was open, and as I neared, I smelled cigarette smoke and heard Ralph's voice rising above the others.

Ralph had perched himself in some chair fit for a king, made of smooth carved wood with a back that stood taller than he did. He was talking about Stalin again, Communism, how property, including the Château de Ferrières, belonged to no one, that it had to be for the use of all people. Ralph was like the underground at Buchenwald, the men who survived perhaps because they were emboldened to fight, to find ways to resist the Nazis any way they could. Perhaps Ralph had it better than I did. I lived by dreams that kept being shattered. He was fueled by his passion.

"Why are we here, then, in the servants' quarters?" a boy called out.

Others around him lifted their fists and shouted out, "Yes, why?"

"We're staying here?" I whispered to the boy closest to me.

He nodded, then informed me that the château was actually off-limits for us boys. We could use the grounds and this house, which was for the servants. Nothing more. "The OSE even brings the meals to us," the boy said.

"Abolish all private property," Ralph cried out in between

taking long drags of his cigarette. "The Rothschilds fled Nazi France, fled to England. They left all the rest of us Jews in Europe to die. To them, we Jews are the poor relations of the family. They are concerned only with their wealth." Ralph hissed, and with that, the room sneered along with him.

"Karl Marx said: 'Under private property . . . each tries to establish over the other an alien power, so as thereby to find satisfaction of his own selfish need,'" Ralph continued.

"Down with the Rothschilds," the boys began to chant, their raised voices bouncing off the walls, causing my ears to ring.

Some of the boys closest to Ralph pushed the wooden bunk beds to the center of the room and stripped them of their mattresses, which some of the other boys began to tear apart. All the while, the room pulsed with boys' voices shouting the mantra: "Stalin! Stalin! For our Father!"

Ralph, perched atop his throne, looked smug as the Hungarian boy who hated Abe and me rolled up some newspaper. Ralph tossed him his lighter, silver, and the Hungarian boy lit paper that had been placed underneath one of the bed frames. Another boy added some of the fabric from the mattresses to the flame.

Quickly, the fire spread. Soon wood was crackling, and the fire was moving toward the curtains.

As smoke filled the servants' quarters, boys pushed one another to escape through the front door, while others, with rags over their faces to avoid inhaling the smoke, added more flammable items to the blaze, including feathers from the pillows, newsprint, and a magazine collection. Soon the room was a painting of reds, oranges, blues, and purples, and all of us having abandoned our differences, standing arm to arm outside, watched the carnage of what we had done.

––––––––

I wasn't sure where the real servants were staying, but they came rushing toward the building, carrying buckets and dragging garden hoses.

The fire was put out without any damage to the structure of the building. But inside was full of smoke, and a couple of the beds and curtains were destroyed. We boys were told to sleep outside with the few blankets we were able to save. Most of us were quiet. I felt it was unsaid among us that we'd finally gone too far.

The next morning, we crept silently to breakfast, where it was served on one of the property's long patios. We then waited, few of us talking.

I didn't see Ralph anywhere. He had left.

Madame Minc, Nini, the professor, and the other OSE staff paced in front of us, like they didn't know what to do. Eventually, they asked us to follow them. Like a parade of ghosts, we twisted through the property, trailing along paths of intricate stonework. Behind us loomed the castle of diamonds and pearls, like a gilded, angry giant glaring its wrath down on us.

We sat cross-legged on the dewy grass and then watched the OSE staff talk some more in whispers to one another, their faces grave. Madame Minc twisted her nose and kept shaking her head, as if the course of action the others wanted was one she didn't agree with. Sitting not far from me were the Intellectuals. I overheard Elie say to one of his friends: "I feel sorry for them. They think they can educate us, and yet the youngest of us knows more than the oldest among them about what exists in the world, of the futility of life, the brutal triumph of death."

There was a new woman in the group, who had arrived shortly before I left for Feldafing. She eventually came forward and shouted that we were going to be separated. Abe leaned over and whispered that the woman's name was Judith, and she had come from the OSE in Switzerland. The boys who wanted kosher food and religious ceremonies and to continue their religious studies were going to a château called Vaucelles in Taverny, Judith said. She then read off the names of the boys going to Taverny, which included the Intellectuals.

Those of us who were between the ages of fourteen and sixteen and didn't want such religious education would go to Le Vésinet.

Judith then went on to say that when we arrived in Le Vésinet, we would commence with a Maccabiah Games. Salek leaned over and explained that the first Maccabiah Games were held in Palestine in 1932, a year after I was born. These were games, like the Olympics, but for Jewish athletes. The Maccabiah Games were named after the Maccabees and in honor of the Bar Kokhba revolts that took place starting in 132 AD. These were rebellions by the Jews of the Roman province of Judea and led by Simeon Bar Kosba against the Roman Empire, which was threatening to build a new city over the ruins of Jerusalem and erect a temple to the Roman god Jupiter on the Temple Mount.

"It's our way of hoping to settle the differences between

you," Judith was saying. "Maybe through sport, you can lay aside those things you feel divide you, unite, and begin moving forward with your lives. We believe in all of you, each and every one of you."

———

A few days later, Abe, Salek, Marek, Joe, and I clambered up the stairs of the sprawling Le Vésinet château that was now our new home and selected a bedroom on the second floor for our own. While the room was smaller than where we'd stayed in Écouis, it seemed the same wooden bunk beds had been brought over.

Le Vésinet, which of course Salek had researched before we arrived, was one of the wealthiest suburbs of Paris. We were about ten miles from downtown Paris, said Madame Minc, who accompanied us to Le Vésinet. Nini and Judith went with the Intellectuals. Salek had discovered that Le Vésinet was also the headquarters of a German intelligence bureau during the Nazi occupation of France. The bureau spied on French civilians and tortured those felt to have information on British soldiers trapped inside France, like paratroopers or airmen whose planes had gone down.

The mansion, like the others on the street, was made of stone and wood, and like in Écouis, the interior was decorated with silky yet well-worn pastel-colored wallpapers. The carpets were shorn, like boots had mowed down the fibers. Red-stained wainscoting gave the place a stuffy feel, like an old man who, when the heavy curtains were drawn back in the mornings, seemed like he was opening his tired eyes.

About fifty of us Buchenwald Boys, many of us from

Poland but not all—in fact, the Hungarian brute who wanted to beat me up was with us—were sent to Le Vésinet, where we were greeted by fifty French Jewish orphans whom the OSE had helped save. The OSE had hidden many Jewish children when the Germans invaded France, often in the south of the country, on farms and in Christian orphanages.

Our first dinner, a welcoming feast, was beef stew and roasted chicken with buttery potatoes. The boys who played instruments performed afterward. There was a cellist among us, and one of the French boys played the piano, a classical piece that he said was composed by Chopin, followed by what he called blues, which he said originated with African slaves in the deep American South and the Caribbean.

When the performance was over, Abe suggested we go outside.

He pulled us close to a newly planted rose bed and asked us all to sit down.

"I have something to tell you," he began.

I shook my head and mumbled "no." I knew before the words escaped his mouth: Abe was leaving.

"To America," he said in a low voice.

"Where?" I asked, swallowing the lump in the back of my throat.

"New York City. An uncle. My father's brother," he said slowly and then more hurriedly, like he felt he owed us an explanation. "My uncle contacted the OSE. He'd been look- ing for me . . . for anyone from the family, once he knew what was happening here . . . here in Europe. He'd been searching all along." Abe rubbed his eyes, smearing his face with dirt.

The five of us fell quiet, but I could sense that our thoughts were all screaming.

Abe was a year older than me. We'd met briefly before we left Częstochowa for Buchenwald. He, too, had been working as a slave laborer for HASAG but in their factory in Kielce, Poland. He was a machinist and at age thirteen was even promoted to foreman. Abe and I became close when I was doused with the burning, exploding meat. From that moment on, we were inseparable.

Abe was born in Łódź on June 10, 1930. He had a brother, Morris, who was two years younger than him. The family escaped the Łódź Ghetto by living in a grandmother's one-room apartment in the town of Nowy Korczyn. The father, to support the family, bought and sold black-market items, and Abe helped in the smuggling operations.

In October 1942, the Germans liquidated Nowy Korczyn of all its Jews. Abe, his brother, grandmother, and mother, along with fifteen other people, fled but were eventually caught. Abe's mother and Abe were sent to work at HASAG. His first job was as an electrician's helper. But like me, his fingers were nimble. He was tiny but strong, and he worked quickly. Unlike me, he was strong-willed and outspoken, quickly gaining promotions because he didn't fear bossing other workers around.

When the Germans started to move the slave laborers from Poland, Abe was sent to Przedbórz, where he was put to work digging anti-tank ditches, then to the HASAG factory at Częstochowa.

At Buchenwald, big Jakow ordered Abe and me to never leave the barracks. But Abe and I liked to sneak out and wander. One day, snow falling like salt flakes, we spied a mound of potatoes, so large, like a giant truck had just emptied its cargo bed on the ground. I don't know why the potatoes weren't moved to a storage room or kitchen, but two SS guards circled the pile, guarding the potatoes, each walking in an opposite direction.

Abe and I hid in between some metal barrels propped up against one of the barracks. We watched and counted right down to the second when, just briefly, both guards disappeared from view. "If we run fast," I whispered to Abe, "we can get in and out without either of them noticing us."

Abe and I argued then, in hushed voices, over who was a quicker runner, not even acknowledging to each other that if we failed in our mission, we would be killed. Finally, being the scrappy kid he was, Abe just ran, leaving me staring after his pumping legs and arms. When he returned, he held in his hand three potatoes.

Back in Block 8, Abe and I removed one of the overhead light bulbs. We then wove a wire through a potato and attached the loose part of the wire to the light socket. When we turned the light switch on, the potato cooked. That night, we pretended those potatoes were lemon cakes and stews full of juicy meat. With every bite, we pretended we were back home, the tables full of endless dishes of food that we tasted and devoured. Hunger has a funny way, I told Abe then, of making the food we did eat seem tastier. "Like our taste buds are aching for anything to remind us of what we used to eat."

"So I leave for America from Cherbourg . . . on a boat . . . to Ellis Island," Abe was saying. "I'm scared, Romek."

"What are you frightened of?" I asked, blinking, focusing on Abe and not our memories.

"What if . . . if I never find my family, Romek?" he said, his voice breaking in and out. "If I go to America, how will they find me?"

"How will I find you?" I found myself asking. Sitting there, looking at Abe, I thought to myself, *How much more can I lose?*

12

IN THE DAYS *leading up to liberation, there was shelling all around Buchenwald.*

American bombs exploded so close the haunches of our barracks shook. A few times, Abe and I could hear the whistling air of the bombs as they descended.

I begged Abe that we should try to escape, to run away, to leave before a bomb fell on top of us. There was no way, I said to Jakow, that we survived all we had to die just before freedom.

On the day before liberation, Jakow informed us that the Nazis had taken 150 of the Jewish boys. The boys were put on a train to nowhere. The SS just wanted the boys dead, evidence of their crimes hidden. Right now it was the most dangerous to be outside, Jakow warned.

In the last breath of night before dawn, when silence was the deepest, Abe, however, agreed to leave with me. How could we know that our freedom was just a few hours ahead? Now was our chance, when everyone, including the SS barracks, was quiet. I didn't need to remind Abe that the watchtower guards might be awake and that they used prisoners who left their barracks at night for target practice: prisoners who needed to urinate or to smoke might as well be dead.

When Abe and I stepped outside, we took some dirt and darkened our faces and the white lines of our pajama clothes, hoping to camouflage ourselves with the night.

As we inched our way forward, almost on tiptoes, toward the metal gate that surrounded our bunker, I saw a flower.

A white flower growing in the mud.

"I think we're dead," I whispered to Abe.

It was cool out. From the dim lights shining from the watchtower, I could see my breath in the air as I spoke.

"Is this heaven?" Abe whispered back, watching his breath, too.

Abe and I stood absolutely still. The silence around us was more frightening, more terrifying than the fear that we would be hit by an American bomb. I whispered to Abe that I wanted to hear Jakow's deep snores and hear Tall Willy's calming voice summoning us to roll call in the morning.

By midafternoon on April 11, 1945, Abe and I were cowering under one of the wooden bed frames, frozen in time, not sure whether we were dead or alive.

Outside were the hurried sounds of feet and the chants and cheers of men.

At one point Jakow shouted across the building that it was safe for all the boys to come out. The underground and resistance had taken over the camp; the SS were gone. The clock above the entrance had been stopped at 3:15 PM: the exact time of our liberation.

All I thought at that moment was that for years, I had woken each morning into a nightmare.

Life was now being presented to me. I had survived.

But what is life? *I thought as I watched the American jeeps make their way into the camp.* What gives life meaning when one is reduced to a number?

"My name is 117098," I told the American soldier when he asked me my name. That's all I was for three years.

I was 117098.

Even the sight of a white flower in mud—hope growing in mud—scared me.

It represented freedom when all I knew was captivity.

―――――

One morning in late August, after the plates and food from breakfast had been cleared away, the OSE staff divided us into teams for the Maccabiah Games. An OSE staff person said the teams were based on our sizes, but we were separated from our friends as well so we could get to know new boys. Abe, Salek, Marek, Joe, and I were all on different teams. The boy from Hungary, who had wanted to beat Abe and me up at Écouis, was on my team. He snarled at me as OSE staff handed out shorts and white undershirts to wear. As we made our way upstairs to change, he nudged me on the stairs. Whatever kindness he had shown that night back in Écouis was gone.

Outside on the mansion's lawn, we sat in our teams. The first order of business, it was announced, was to come up with a team name. Huddled together, none of my team members or I spoke. We eyed one another up and down with suspicion. Finally, a boy from Warsaw shouted out a team name. The rest of us shrugged. None of us cared. We then had to write our team name on a large placard that the boy from Warsaw carried as we paraded onto a nearby soccer field for the opening ceremonies of the games.

An OSE staff person officially started the games by outlining the rules of fairness, camaraderie, and sportsmanship that we were all to follow. The games were not about winning but about supporting one another. The sporting events would be running, jumping, soccer, sledding on the grasses of a small hill, leaping from tree to tree with ropes, and other team events.

I loved the running competitions, and I made it to the semifinals of one of the mid-distance races. But I lost to Abe, who quickly outran me. He actually ended up winning not just that race but the two short-distance races as well.

My team didn't do so well on the soccer pitch. We weren't united. Each of us would aim to take the ball and run it alone, instead of passing. The other team was doing much the same. Boys on both sides hissed not only at the players on the opposing teams but also at one another. The score was 0–0 with just two minutes left in the game. That's when the Hungarian boy turned to me and said he'd had enough of this. His competitive streak ran stronger than his urge to hurt me and the other Polish boys. He started moving down the field with the ball. Just as he was to be intercepted, he passed the ball to the boy from Warsaw, who then passed it to me, where I was standing right in front of the goalpost. I kicked and scored. We won the game. When the whistle blew, my team gave one another the thumbs-up and V-for-victory signs with our hands, then hugged our competitors. Something in that

Buchenwald Boys taking part in the Maccabiah Games put on by the OSE.

moment had shattered: our hatred, perhaps. We began to see one another as extensions of ourselves.

Relays followed, one of which involved three-legged races. The Hungarian boy and I joined forces and won.

In a running relay race, we saw ourselves falling down on top of each other, laughing because we couldn't pass the baton without dropping it. Suddenly, all of us, on every team, began to laugh and help one another.

For the soccer finals, of which my team was thrown out in the quarterfinals, we sat close together and watched, cheering both sides as goals were scored and sighing during missed passes.

At the end of the second day, before the closing ceremonies, we all linked arms and did the hora. Then we stood still and sang the Buchenwald song.

When the day awakens,
Ere the sun smiles,
The gangs march out to the day's toils
Into the breaking dawn.
And the forest is black and the heavens red,
In our sacks we carry a piece of bread
And in our hearts, in our hearts—sorrow.
O Buchenwald, I cannot forget you,
For you are my fate.
He who has left you, he alone can measure
How wonderful freedom is!
O Buchenwald, we do not whine and wail,
And whatever our fate,
We will say yes to life,
For the day will come when we are free . . .

––––––

On Abe's last night, Madame Minc had the cooks make pierogi stuffed with mushroom and cabbage—Polish food—and for dessert, honey pastries that tasted, Abe said, just like his mama's, bringing tears to his eyes. The Polish boys who could play instruments and sing that night performed Polish folk songs. As I listened, my mind drifted off, remembering when Jakow would pick up an accordion or a fiddle, once even a flute, and play similar songs. Before everyone else went to bed, the Polish boys sang "God Save Poland," "Boże, coś Polskę."

Abe and I remained awake. Sitting on chairs in the dining room, sipping tea, we talked about Buchenwald.

"Remember the Red Cross packages?" he asked at one point.

I sure did.

The underground at Buchenwald had arranged for the Red Cross packages the political inmates would receive to be given to the children instead. Grown men, starving men, were more than eager to hand over these packages of canned meats, sugar candies, warm socks, and oversize hand-knit sweaters once they knew they were going to boys, some as young as seven. When Abe and I got our packages, we tore into the boxes, tossing out onto the bed the contents, which included bandages and pairs of ear warmers, until we found what we were looking for: chocolate. Neither of us had had chocolate or any form of dessert since Germany invaded Poland. We carefully pulled apart the gold wrappings and then laid the chocolate bars out in front of us. After admiring the chocolate for a while, we cautiously, sure it was a trick and we'd open our eyes and the chocolate would be gone, picked up our bars. We both licked the chocolate like ice cream, too afraid to bite into the bar, our gums sore and our teeth loose and rotting from malnutrition.

I didn't want Abe to go, but I knew he had to.

13

I OVERSLEPT.

I quickly looked over to see that Abe's bedding had been stripped. The worn leather-bound brown suitcase in which he had packed his few belongings, including prints of his photos taken in Écouis, was gone.

I leaped out of bed, panicked. Not bothering to do up the laces of my shoes, I skirted down the staircase, taking two, three, even four steps at a time, running at full speed, to the dining room. He wasn't there. Madame Minc said he'd left, but if I hurried, I could catch up to him at the train station.

My legs soon became strained, my muscles sore, from my running. I could feel a blister bubbling on one of my heels. Somehow, though, I made it, breathless and wheezing, to the station.

It was early morning, and a large crowd of French commuters was pushing its way onto the platforms.

I wove in between and ducked through them, but I couldn't find Abe anywhere. Jumping up and down to see over and through the bodies, I started calling out Abe's name. A train arrived, quickly swallowing up most of the crowd, and I was left alone on the platform.

My shoulders slumped, and I sighed. I had missed him. I might never see him again.

"Romek," I heard a voice call. I looked up to see Abe standing on the opposite platform. The professor was beside him. Abe and Professor Manfred waved for me to join them. I started to climb down the platform wall to cross the tracks when a train conductor walking past grabbed the scruff of my neck and pulled me up. He pointed toward the exit. In Yiddish, I explained, while pointing, that I needed to get to my friend on the other side of the tracks. The conductor snapped something back at me in French, his nostrils flaring, his eyes wild.

"You can't cut across the track," the professor called out. "It could electrocute you. We will wait for you."

By the time I made it to Abe, I was crawling on my knees from fatigue. Abe fell into my arms. His soft and round flesh felt warm and familiar.

"The professor says you can come to see me off," he said when he pulled away. I looked into his face. His cheeks, like mine, were soaked in tears. "It will be a journey, maybe the last we take together."

Abe was taking a ship from Cherbourg, a port that had just reopened after being destroyed during the Allied invasion of France. I'd never been to the sea before, seen the ocean, or smelled such scents of seaweed and the fresh, salty breeze. The light on the northern coast of France seemed fainter, the sky higher, the birdsong distant, like their voices were moving up toward heaven, not down to earth like rain.

The ship was so large that standing close to it, I couldn't see where it started and where it ended. I would make paper boats that I would sail on the Kamienna River. None compared to this ship. People, many of them men in American Army uniforms, had already boarded. They were leaning over the deck railings, waving.

For me, America was John Wayne, the Hollywood movie star whose movies I'd watched with Polish subtitles back in Skarżysko-Kamienna. I couldn't picture this New York City that Abe said was just as big if not bigger than Paris, with buildings taller than the Eiffel Tower, stretching all the way up to the clouds.

Standing off to the side, Abe opened his leather suitcase and pulled out one of the shirts he had selected off the truck in Écouis. He handed it to me. "This was the first thing I owned," he said, passing me the shirt. "It was the first thing that was mine since I left Łódź. I want you to have it."

I shuddered, for I hadn't thought to bring anything for him.

"You know why I ran for the potatoes?" he then asked.

"Because you're stubborn and always have to be right!" I chided.

"No," he said, his face serious. "Because my little brother was sent to the chambers. I know it, and I didn't want to lose another brother."

I gasped then, realizing I, too, thought of Abe as a brother.

"I didn't have a dream that I would be going home to my family the way you did," he continued. "I didn't have a dream to get me through. I didn't have any way of knowing if Papa or my brother was alive, not the way you did. But your dream, that you would walk into your house where everyone was waiting for you, that dream kept me going. I survived because of your dream. You helped me believe."

"All of us boys probably had something inside us that got us through. We all had to find something to survive," I said, hugging Abe.

My eyes stayed on Abe as he walked up the boat plank. Eventually he became a speck as he merged with the American Army men. I waved nonetheless, waved until my arms were sore. The professor and I stood there while the boat tooted that it was about to leave. We were still standing there, staring, as that giant vessel made its way out of the harbor toward the English Channel, headed to the ocean.

———

Every day, we boys at Le Vésinet were learning of the deaths of family members, friends, and neighbors from our cities and villages. Most of the news came by way of people visiting the center and were rumors, but as the news we listened to on the radio at night reported on the increasing scale of what the Nazis had done to Europe's Jewry, we all suspected the information to be true. Sometimes, the information was factual, coming from Nazi archives collected at the concentration camps and being deciphered by Allied intelligence workers. That's when Madame Minc would call the boy into her office and gently break the news. We all seemed to breathe a sigh of relief when it was not our name called. We moaned and cried and comforted those who heard their mama had been killed, their sister, brother, papa. We all waited anxiously and nervously, knowing our turn was coming. Most of us had wanted to hang on to the hope that we were the lucky ones.

Joe, Marek, and Salek were studying now, with teachers brought into Le Vésinet. Learning was I guess their way of forgetting the tension we lived with daily. Their lessons were French and math, with the goal that once they had mastered the language and were where they would be academically had they stayed in school, they would then go into a French classroom with other children. In the afternoons, social workers came to talk to us boys. Divided into small groups, sitting in semicircles on stiff, creaky wooden chairs, we boys would listen to the men and women talking about the opportunities for schooling, vocational training, and immigration to France or other countries that were available to us. The social workers were supposed to encourage us boys to talk about our futures. But few of us did so. We'd sit there silently, twitching and flinching in our seats, until someone blurted out some experience from the ghettos or the death camps. That got us talking. We all wanted to share our stories.

I didn't like studying, not the way Joe, Marek, and Salek did. My mind would drift in class. One day, I started thinking of my school friends back in Poland, Halinka and Wiesiek, a sister and brother, born a year apart. They were also our neighbors, living a few houses down from mine on the Third of May Street. At Christmas, I would go to their house and sing carols and decorate their Christmas tree with strings of popcorn and angel and star ornaments their mama made out of shortbread. At Easter, we decorated eggs in their kitchen in bright blues, reds, and purples. During the Jewish holidays, Halinka and Wiesiek would come to my house and eat cholent, listen to our prayers and Papa's stories.

But one day in the spring of 1938, just before Easter, on our way home from school, our arms usually locked together as we skipped, Halinka and Wiesiek and some of the other children from my class pushed me down the side of a small hill. They kicked my stomach, pulled my hair, slapped my face, and spat into my eyes. These children, who were my classmates, my friends, who had never shown any aggression or anger toward me or anyone else, had become different people. They eventually left me there, crying, bloodied, and bruised, saying my people had killed Jesus. I limped home. There Mama cradled me in her arms and Chaim took me to the doctor, where I learned I had a broken arm.

I suspected why my classmates had done this to me. I was Jewish and not like them. A few times a week, our teacher, a stern woman who rarely smiled, would ask the Jewish boys in the class to leave. We'd run up and down the hallway of smoothed stained wood, sliding in our socks, while the Christian children had religion class. Once I sat by the door and listened. The students were being taught the Catholic prayer for the pernicious Jews, "pernicious" meaning people who have a bad effect on others.

———

"Let us pray also for the faithless Jews: that Almighty God may remove the veil from their hearts; so that they too may acknowledge Jesus Christ our Lord. Almighty and eternal God, who dost not exclude from thy mercy even Jewish faithlessness: hear our prayers, which we offer for the blindness of that people . . ."

Nearing Good Friday, the Christian children were asked to pray for our conversion to Christianity.

When school resumed after Easter, Halinka and Wiesiek

showed up at our door to walk to school with me. They acted like nothing had happened. That was the start of the shattering of my world, of my innocent childhood, where people, even children, could be one thing one day and then something else on another. That was the day I saw myself as different. From that day on, I didn't trust anyone except my family . . . and soon I would lose faith in even them.

Then came along Jakow and Tall Willy. And Abe.

Always my thoughts were on Abe. Did he make it safely to America? Did he like his uncle? Did he get lots of food?

After class one day, Marek, suspecting my boredom or malaise, my thoughts that tumbled like weeds in a windstorm, suggested we go into Paris in search of Ralph and Communists. I had always seen Marek as a hanger-on. He was never the first to speak, and he never really said much at all. He just agreed with Salek, like he was Salek's sidekick.

Ralph hadn't shown his face since the Château de Ferrières fire. I wondered if he had picked up with Gustav, who had fled, rumor had it, to Berlin, where he was going to open a bar and raise money to help the Buchenwald Boys start their own businesses when they were ready.

But Marek reminded me of the jazz bars, where Ralph said he'd meet up with other people like him. "Maybe he is still here in France?" Marek suggested.

We boys had been given French Army veteran pins, allowing us to travel the trains and go to concerts, clubs, and movies for free. Marek and I wore ours on the collar of our shirts.

The train station was a few blocks away and involved our

walking through a partly residential area before merging into the main section of the suburb.

As we walked, I looked at the homes, several floors tall, with big, painted wooden doors and large windows, some still broken from the war, patched up with tape and cardboard. Near the station, I could see the scars of propaganda posters informing the French Jews that they weren't allowed in certain places. Pieces of these posters were still tacked to bulletin boards and lampposts.

On the train, Parisian women wore pencil-tight skirts with matching tailored jackets, bright lipstick, and hats, which I imagined Papa would admire for their intricate sewing. The perfumes and colognes of the women and men wafted over me: lavender and lilac that I remembered I would go out into the fields with Golda to look for. She'd made fabric sachets, filling them with the herbs that she would hang around the house and place inside our pillowcases.

Parisian men wore suits with high waists, wide-bottom pants, and large creases. Around their necks were silk scarves. Their hair was slicked back like Ralph wore his and unparted. But it wasn't just their bright, fashionable clothes and sense of style that struck me as odd. It was the smiles on the Parisians' faces. The air of lightness that floated around them. It was the way Mama and Papa would speak to our neighbors as they passed one another on Third of May Street, the way the butcher would banter back and forth with Chaim about how big he was getting or the baker would rave about the Jewish holidays.

Marek and I huddled in close together. I suspected he felt like he was out of place, too. I recalled then something Elie had said before he left us for his new home. Speaking of us boys, he said: "We long to remain faithful to the dead."

Out on the Paris street, people walked quickly.

There was a skip in their steps. I felt lost in the busyness of it all. But Marek seemed to know where he was going as he led me up sloping streets in an area he said was called Montmartre. Marek said Montmartre was an area of Paris known for its artists, including famous painters and musicians. As the hair on my arms stood up on end and beads of sweat dripped down my back and my eyes watered, Marek led me like we were in an obstacle course through the Paris crowds and twisting cobblestone streets and alleyways until we stopped in front of a jazz club.

He had me follow him down some stone steps into a darkened room, lit by tiny candles set on low tables. "It's a jazz bar," Marek whispered, like I couldn't tell it was a music club.

There was piano music, chaotic and fast, not like the Beethoven symphonies Papa would listen to on our phonograph or classical music the guest musicians would play in Écouis. Out of nowhere, a female voice started singing. It was high-pitched but clear, like crystal.

As Marek and I wove through the room, in and out of men and women smoking cigarettes and drinking something in clear glasses, a sensation I hadn't felt before moved through me. I finally saw the singer and the pianist. She was performing in French, only a few words of which I could make out. But just her voice, this type of music, woke something inside me, and it was like I could understand everything she was saying. I almost felt like crying. Ralph had been right. Language separated us. Here, with jazz, I was experiencing something rare, where language didn't matter.

A Black woman was dressed in an off-white sleeveless dress, long, with a low waist, and attached to the fabric were shimmering broaches in an array of jewels. I stopped walking then, staring at the glittering diamonds, remembering Mama's silver earrings and the family photographs that had been sewn into the lining of my jacket I wore at HASAG.

The Nazis, before they moved the Jewish families to the ghetto, had come to all our homes, ransacking the cupboards and taking anything of value. Mama's crystal glasses, silver spoons, good china, and silver Kiddush cups were all carted away. But Mama and Papa had sewn złoty, photographs of each of us, and Mama's few jewels into the linings of our coats. Among the photographs was one of me as a baby; another of Mama and Papa; a third of my entire family, including one of Golda and Nathan that had been taken by the Skarżysko-Kamienna photographer just months before the Germans invaded Poland; and one of Chaim in his Polish military uniform.

I knew enough that the jewels on the singer's dress were not real.

Beside the singer, a Black man was sitting on a stool, his fingers seeming to float over the piano keys, like he wasn't really playing at all.

I remembered Buchenwald then. A few days after liberation, the American Army's 183rd Engineer Combat Battalion arrived, made up entirely of Black soldiers. Everyone at

Buchenwald was white. Jakow had said these men were treated very badly, that in America they had laws segregating Blacks from most of society, much like the Nazis did us Jews. But still these men were fighting for their country, committed to ending a war and liberating people oppressed just like they were, Jakow had said.

Now I was staring at not only a Black piano player who performed like the spirit of music itself was moving through him but a Black woman, whose voice seemed to shine a light on the dusty cobwebs inside me.

Marek sat down at one of the tables off to the side of the stage. He waved for me to join him and then patted the vacant seat beside him. As I neared, I studied the back of the man sitting at the table with Marek: the tweed jacket in the summer heat that was never taken off, styled hair curled around the ear ever so slightly in the humidity. Professor Manfred. He was smoking a cigarette, tapping a foot, and swaying his head to the music. When I approached the table, I saw that his eyes were closed and his jaw slightly raised. Any anger I had had at first seeing him there left like it was sucked up by a vacuum.

The professor looked like peace. And something else moved through me then as well: he understood the music, too.

14

WHEN THE OVERHEAD lights of the jazz club came on, I watched as the patrons started to pile out, making room for those wanting to catch the evening performance.

Soon it was just Marek, the professor, the staff, and me.

It dawned on me what was going on. Marek had brought me here on purpose. I kicked him under the table, giving him a long look, my eyes trying to ask him: "Why is the professor here?"

Marek blushed, and he mumbled that he had to go to the washroom, leaving me alone with the professor.

"I have been wanting to talk to you," the professor finally said.

I ignored him. Instead, I let my eyes flit around the room. In the dim light, the place looked otherworldly, like a magical cavern under the sea. Now, with all the lights on bright, it looked run-down. The ceiling was cracked in places; some of the lights on the chandeliers were burned out or nonexistent; the floors were scuffed.

The professor reached over and took my wrist. "Romek, I know you think all of us with the OSE can't imagine what you've been through, that we're ridiculous to care, that we can't reach you where you now live, but you're wrong," he said, leaning in close.

I continued to look away. I didn't want to be touched. My body flinched to pull my arm back. But something inside stopped me from doing so. Instead, I dug my fingernails in hard to the palms of my hands. "What could you possibly know?" I eventually snapped in a low voice. I was searching the faces of the staff now, looking for signs that one of them might be a Communist or, better yet, Ralph. That was my future. "Stalin," I wanted to tell the professor, even as I thought to myself, "What does a Communist look like?" I had only ever seen them at Buchenwald, in their camp pajamas with the red badges they wore. I couldn't imagine what they would look like having gained weight and wearing civilian clothes. Did they look like Ralph?

I'd made up my mind, right then and there. I was going to join the Communists and go back to Eastern Europe. I would find the Buchenwald Boys who had already left to join Communist movements in Russia, Hungary, and Romania.

"In July 1942, the French police came to the apartment building where I lived with my wife and my daughter, who would be, if alive, about the same age as you," the professor was saying. "Behind these men was the concierge for our building, an older man who used to give my daughter butterscotch candies. Are you listening, Romek?"

My eyes still scanning the room, I grunted that I was listening.

"In 1940, the Germans had ordered Jews to register with their local police. Before that, France didn't have citizens list their religion. One of the policemen was carrying a list of names and started to read off mine, my wife's, my daughter's. He then said we had a few minutes to pack. My wife started crying. I pleaded to know where we were going. I knew that since the Germans took over Paris, Jews were not safe. Signs appeared almost immediately saying Jews were forbidden in public parks, on certain streets, eventually outside our homes except for a certain time of the day when we were allowed to get food from the stores. Even then, since it was late in the day, most of the rations in the shops were long gone, taken by the Parisians. There were rumors coming out of Germany of camps for Jews and roundups, of businesses destroyed, of the stripping of all rights. But I had no idea . . ." His voice trailed away. He took off his glasses then, which had steamed, and cleaned them with a tissue.

"My family and I were ordered to get on a bus that was waiting outside—a typical Paris bus but now filled with other Jews, some of whom I knew from synagogue, others from the university," he continued.

"We were taken to the Vélodrome d'Hiver stadium, which was a cycle track. We lived there for months, the toilets being the very spots where we sat, ate, and slept, drinking in one another's stenches, desperate for water, for food, for information about what was happening to us. Babies started to die in their mothers' arms, and the old just turned stiff. Some jumped to their deaths. Finally, we were taken to Auschwitz-Birkenau. I was in Auschwitz. I worked. My wife and child were sent to Birkenau, the gas chambers."

I finally turned and was looking at the professor. He had taken off his tweed jacket and rolled up a sleeve. On his arm was a number. His Auschwitz concentration-camp number.

In a hushed voice, I told the professor about when I'd gotten my number. It was the night Chaim had taken me to work at HASAG. A Lithuanian soldier supporting the Nazis gave me a slip of paper that he said was my name from then on. It had my number on it. 117098.

As I continued to look at the professor, I saw something I hadn't before: his sagging shoulders, tired eyes, sinking jowls. I saw the frayed ends of his shirt collar and the worn patches on his tweed coat. Like in the ghetto, when a gray hair would fall out from underneath Mama's headscarf or I'd see the dark circles under her eyes that she tried to conceal using Golda's face powder, these tiny things revealed the professor's vulnerabilities, the face he wasn't showing the world, the one he tried to hide.

Marek returned carrying three orange sodas that he said the bartender had given him for free. I wiped the tears from my face and, with a shaking hand, took a long drink. When I was done, the professor started talking again.

"*Meine tayer kindern*" (my dear children), the professor said. "All of us who survived are left in a million tiny pieces. I have entire days where I am not sure what is real and what is unreal. But if we don't go into the sorrow and see what is behind it, Romek, we will be destroyed." He was now directing his conversation just toward me. "What would your parents want for you?" He then leaned in and asked me in such a low voice, I had to strain to hear. "I've asked you this before, but now I really want you to answer. What would your parents want for you?"

I drew quiet.

The professor sat back in his chair, sipping his drink and then lighting up another cigarette.

I pinched my eyes shut tight as images of the camps came to me. The men at Buchenwald I would see being taken away, injected with some chemical or experimental medicine, returning to the barracks lost, dazed, dying. The *Muselmann* prisoners, those ghosts of the camp, the men who had drifted off to death long before their bodies died. These men would eventually run into the electric fences or just abandon their work, knowing they would be shot. I saw in front of me the people ripped apart by the dogs. I even felt the cold showers I had been forced to take in winter. And afterward, being made to line up outside for roll call, sometimes naked. 117098, that was who I had become. 117098. And to survive, I had to forget everything and just be that number, do what was asked of me, nothing else.

"What would your parents want for you?" the professor asked again.

I recalled a dinner then, when Papa was quizzing me in math. At school, we had just started learning the times tables. I was a natural. The only counting I had done since the ghetto, though, was count the number of camps I'd been in, six; the numbers of SS, Gestapo, soldiers from other countries; the numbers of shots puncturing the air, letting me know how many were killed; the number of footsteps coming toward me and how many it took for them to walk away. At the start of the war, the soldiers seemed to shoot and shoot, not even caring whether their bullets killed, maimed, or missed. But by the end of the war, when Jakow said the bullets were running out, it was just shoot to kill. I counted also the words used to describe us Jews. *Untermenschen* (subhuman). We were *untermenschen*. I realized that I had started to believe the very things I was told. I was a rat and worm food. As long as I could work, my heart could remain beating.

"You are the baby of our family," Mama would say. "You can do anything you want in this world, and anything you do will make us proud."

"I like numbers," I finally whispered to the professor. "I was good at math."

Marek, the professor, and I were quiet on the train back to Le Vésinet. In my mind, I saw falling leaves; I saw myself playing tag with Moishe along the river, kicking a football that Chaim had made out of twisting together pieces of string and some of Papa's fabric from his shop. I heard Papa reading the story of Moses from the Haggadah, his voice deep, moving through our small house like a heavy wind. I felt his strong embrace at the synagogue as he wrapped me inside his tallit. I smelled Mama, her scent of flour and the wildflowers she would pick and place in a vase that had been her mama's.

It was dark when we got off the train. The days were getting shorter. Autumn was on its way. As the three of us walked back to the mansion, the only light that marked our way came from oval amber bulbs set high on black metal lampposts and from the windowsills of homes where the curtains had not been drawn.

In Skarżysko-Kamienna, there were not so many houses or buildings like in France, and they weren't built so close together. I could walk out my front door and see the night sky stretching from one end of the horizon to the other.

I realized then that I had looked at the sky only once after the Germans came to Poland. And that was the day I was put on the truck to be sent to the woods to be shot.

I wanted to look at the sky now.

A few houses from the mansion, I wandered onto someone's property, a lawn that flowed from near the house into an untrimmed garden, and lay on my back. I stared up at the stars. There weren't many, not like in Skarżysko on cloudless nights. The lights of Paris shone a veil that covered many of the stars and all of the Milky Way. But there were still some, one maybe even a planet, that hung bright.

I stretched my arms and legs out like I would do when making snow angels in the winter.

And that's when I heard it. Mama's voice tickling my ear. "Without night, there would be no morning," she had told me when I could no longer go to the regular school with the Polish children. And when *cheder* was canceled because the Nazis said Jewish children were more useless than their German pigs, which at least they could eat, "Always walk toward the light," she had said.

"Why did I forget these things about my home?" I whispered, hoping the star that hung the brightest could hear me. What struck me then was that these stars always shone, even when we were in the camps—beacons leading us home.

"Stars," I murmured. "That's one thing the Nazis couldn't destroy."

Some of the boys.

15

IN MY DREAM, I'm with the partisans again.

The partisan boys lit a fire that, in late winter, should not have spread the way it did, catching the skeletal and brittle branches of trees overhead. It should have died quickly in the damp air and melting snow.

The partisans were wild-eyed this night, drunker than usual, slurring their words, their eyes dancing toward me with that same look of disgust as the SS and guards at HASAG.

"Dance, Jew boy," the yellow-haired boy said, his upper lip turning into a snarl.

He shot his pistol, grazing my shoulder.

As some branches over the heads of the partisans crackled and began to rain sparks down on us, the boys' attention wavered.

I didn't think twice. As they were looking up, I ran, thanking the spreading fire for giving me a window to escape.

Slipping in the mud and ice, I skirted in and out of trees, leaped over logs and boulders, and ran right through shallow

streams, breaking the ice where it had not yet melted, my feet
sinking into the cold water.

By the time I made it back to the outskirts of the HASAG
barracks, my boots were caked in mud and wet, like they'd
been swimming. I was sure my toes had frostbite.

I hunched down low, in some prickly bushes that left burs
on my clothes and scratched my skin, waiting until morning,
until the guards changed and the electric fence would be off
for a few minutes.

I then snuck my way back in, using my nails and a stick to
dig a small tunnel under the fence because I didn't have any
jewels or złoty to bribe a guard to hold it up for me. I crept
through to the other side.

Back.

I was back. Inside.

A prisoner of the Germans.

I can't say if I had renewed enthusiasm for life; I just knew I'd
settled into a routine.

I began eating my food with cutlery, not my fingers. I was
one of the last boys at the center to do so. I found I didn't even
remember at first how to hold a fork or cut a piece of meat
with a knife. Salek had to show me. At Buchenwald, when
the Americans came, we had food. Soldiers passed out sar-
dines and bread, beans and chocolate. When Abe and I
received our rations, we started to dig in, only to have Jakow
come up behind us and order us to spit it out. He took our
food and said he would give it to us slowly, in pieces. If we
ate too fast or too much, with our shrunken stomachs and

stomach and intestine muscles not used to working, we could get very sick, unable to digest the food. He was right. A few of the boys who did not have that warning died. Many were sick. The camp filled with our vomit.

Once our stomachs returned to our being able to eat three meals a day, most of us boys stuffed food into our mouths, huge handfuls, swallowing unchewed pieces of meat and vegetables. Salek also showed me how to take small portions of food at a time and chew. It was like I was a baby learning how to eat all over again.

Most of my clothes were covered in grease stains from wiping my hands on them, and the staff found me new clothes. I placed my old clothes in a metal container on the property used for burning leaves and watched the fabric and whatever remnants of lice and fleas I still carried with me from Buchenwald go up in flames.

I started sleeping in real pajamas, and every Thursday, I sent my clothes to be laundered. I was even wearing underwear again, a different pair every day.

When my family and I lived in the ghetto, Mama tried to keep us all clean, washing our clothes in well water, if she could get enough, that she'd boil if we could find wood for the stove, and hanging them on a clothesline off the balcony to dry. In the winter, the pants legs would be frozen stiff like she'd washed the legs that wore the pants, too.

At Buchenwald, Jakow made Abe and me and the other boys in our barracks bathe. He would force us to follow him, single file, to the showers, which were icy cold. With the same soap we used on our bodies, Jakow then made us wash our clothes under the shower faucet. We would walk around naked, even in winter, until our clothes dried. Jakow, though, would try and distract us from our shivers and chattering teeth by picking up his story of the princess or telling us another folk story.

Now, like eating, I had to relearn how to bathe and wash my hair. I'd never had a bath before, not in a full-size bathtub, and slipped into the warm waters, often staying well past my turn, with other boys banging on the door to be let in. The first time I bathed, I used a bar of white soap, lathering up the suds on a cloth and then scrubbing every part of my body. But I was still not clean. That time, I had to wash and refill the tub three times before I got all the dirt off, watching each time as the water swirled around the drain, at first black from the years of dirt that hung on me like icing on one of Mama's cakes, then gray to light brown and finally clear. I also used a nailbrush to dig deep under my nails to remove the grime and mud that were still there from Buchenwald. After each bath, I would look in the mirror, staring at my eyes, the shape of my nose, my square jawline, the wrinkles, my burn scars, searching for any recognition of my family. "Who am I?" I whispered. Despite that it was nearly a year now since liberation, I still thought of myself as 117098 first, Romek second.

"Identity," Salek said one night as we sat talking in our dorm room, the lights off, as we had all become secure that mornings would follow nights and that our nightmares weren't real. "That's what the Nazis took from us: who we were and are."

"They took away our humanity," Marek grumbled. I nodded.

"Our trust in others, our belief in life and people, our memories. All gone," Joe said with a sigh.

In the evenings, the four of us would scramble for seats in front of the radio. I grabbed hold of the good news stories of Allied forces and civilians finding groups of Jews alive, hidden in crypts underneath churches, in tunnels, in caverns and sewer systems below towns and cities. Some Jews were even found in canyons deep in forests, and that made me think of the partisans. I guess there were good partisan groups, too.

I was discovering there were good people out there. The Nazis didn't destroy everyone.

Professor Manfred became my mentor.

All of us boys had someone either assigned to us or an adult we gravitated toward who guided us. For most of the other boys, the mentorship came in the way mostly of school, as some of them by January 1946 were even attending French primary school and figuring out a vocation.

But before I could even start real school, I had to take a test to see which grade I should be in. I started to pay attention in my classes as I realized I was falling behind. The professor and I did a lot of one-on-one meetings in cafés, and when the warmer weather floated around us, in spring 1946, the parks became our tutorial rooms. By then I was reading French comic books, including *The Adventures of Tintin*. The professor and I also went to French movies.

Buchenwald Boys were leaving pretty regularly, to be reunited with relatives, most of whom lived in far-off countries, but a few went to live with family members in Europe who had survived the Nazis' mass murder.

On the actual anniversary of our one-year liberation from Buchenwald, we boys who remained were told we could have a party, a birthday party, as many of us thought of April 11 as our second birthday. Madame Minc had the cooks bake giant chocolate cakes with gooey frosting. But most of us were somber. None of us really felt like celebrating.

A few days later, at Passover, sitting on a bench in the Jardin des Tuileries, the professor asked if I could read the story of Moses's exodus from Egypt. He passed me a well-worn, leather-bound copy of the Haggadah, which he said had been in his family for several generations. In the part read by children, his daughter had been the one to do all the roles.

As I flipped through the pages, Buchenwald and Rabbi Herschel Shachter came to my mind. Not long after liberation, the chaplain with the US Army's VIII Corps had coordinated a Shabbat, transforming the Buchenwald movie theater into a synagogue. Some, including the Intellectuals, sat as close as they could to the front and actively took part. Others went through the motions, Abe told me afterward. And still others, like me, didn't even show up. Not long after that, the rabbi handed out prayer books. For many of us, those prayer books were the first thing we had owned in years. I held mine tightly, thinking, *Mine. Animals don't own things. Now I do. I am no longer an animal.* However, Baruch Goldberg, one of the Jewish brickmason teachers, took the books back. He threw some against a wall, shouting at the boys: "You would accept prayer books and pray after your parents went up the chimneys in the camps? Where was God then?"

My eyes wandered from the Haggadah to the boys and then the professor as I slowly shook my head.

"I'm not ready," I whispered, remembering Ralph and the Communists at Buchenwald, their belief that we were all equal and that religion only separated us. "If I hadn't been Jewish," I whispered to the professor, "I'd be home in Poland with my family right now."

———

One late afternoon, walking back from a café with the professor, I spied the girl with the red hair I'd seen on the train coming home from Feldafing.

My heart skipped, and I blinked, thinking at first I was seeing a mirage. How could she be there?

But as I drew closer, I could see it was her. She was working in the front garden where I had lain to look at the stars. The garden was a mess of weeds and overgrown bushes. She and a woman were tossing dead leaves left over from autumn into a metal bin. As I passed the girl, she looked up. Our eyes locked. Shy, I quickly looked away. When I looked up again, her eyes were still glued to me. I saw flash across her face what I thought was a smile. She recognized me, too.

As spring unfolded into summer's muted golden and blue hues, I'd leave the professor after our studies to walk by the girl's house. She was often in her garden, which slowly was being transformed as she planted wildflowers, daffodils, daisies, and carnations. Sometimes, she held a small magnifying glass and seemed to be studying the petals. By the end of July, her garden was a painter's palette of flowers in pinks, yellows, deep violets, and even blues.

One evening after dinner, I went for a walk in search of the girl. She was there in her garden, wearing a white dress with puffy sleeves and rubber boots.

I mustered up the strength to approach her. As I moved in her direction, I was confident at first. But then I turned sheepish. I stood out on the street just watching her, my legs unable to move despite my mind telling me to turn back. Again I felt this knowing inside me, like I had met this girl before. Then she saw me and motioned for me to come closer. I suddenly felt self-conscious of my appearance: my thinness, my Jewishness, my ragged clothes and sullen, scared face. The words "worm food" and "pigs are more useful than you Jews" that the Nazis would spit out ricocheted through my mind. As I inched toward her, I was certain this girl would be disgusted with me when she saw me up close.

When I was near enough to touch her, I saw that she wore a silver necklace with a tiny Star of David. She blushed and tucked the necklace into her shirt. "I'm not supposed to show people," she whispered in French. Now she looked nervous, her face strained, her eyes shifting. "It was my mother's."

I realized then that she, too, had a story. She, too, had heard these Nazi words.

My French was good enough that we could have a conversation. She introduced herself as Aurore. "Romek," I pushed out, fighting the urge to tell her my number.

"Romek," she repeated. "I like the name. I have never heard it before."

"It's Polish," I said. "My Hebrew name is Rachmil."

She showed me what she was doing. With her magnifying glass, she was looking at the bees that nested in the ground.

She showed me the elaborate dome-like nests. I could see bees burrowing inside.

––––––––

"Do you ever think you're losing your mind?" I asked the professor a few days later, when we finished a lesson on French verbs and conjugations and were licking ice creams, mine mint flavored.

The professor had just said that my studies were progressing quickly. If I kept things up, I could possibly start regular French school in September. I was now reading children's chapter books in French, and I knew my times tables, some division and algebra.

"I can't see their faces anymore," I continued. "I can't remember what they looked like."

"Your family?" he asked.

I nodded.

"I know, Romek. Me too."

"The night Chaim took me to work at HASAG, he had sewed photographs and złoty into the lining of my coat. He told me the photos were to remember, the money and jewels to bribe the guards for extra food or a blanket. Every night before . . . ," I started, then paused, tilting my head to the side, remembering. "I'd look at the photo of Mama and Papa and the photo of my entire family.

"When the Nazis moved us west toward Germany, I still had my jacket with the photographs and money inside. But at Częstochowa, I was ordered to strip, placing all my clothes onto a pile with others'. I then went into a shower." I stopped and started as my mind replayed the images of that day like a movie in slow motion. All of us prisoners had heard rumors about the Nazi showers, that they were killing rooms. That from the faucets, instead of water, the chemical Zyklon-B would spill out, choking all life from us. Us former HASAG work slaves, we shook and held one another, naked, as we walked into the shower room, our bare feet sloshing in the mud outside. Some men recited the Kaddish, believing we were about to die. When the water came, many laughed. Even though the water was freezing, men tilted their heads up toward the faucets with smiles they had not worn and would not wear again for months, if not years.

When we emerged from the showers, the guards ordered us all to put on new clothes. In front of us were piles of slacks and billowy shirts, concentration-camp pajamas, not the clothes we'd been previously wearing. Someone beside me whispered that the linings of our jackets were probably being ripped apart right now so the Nazis could line their own pockets with our jewels and money and burn anything else.

Burn my photographs.

"I don't have any pictures of my family, either." The professor's voice pressed into my memories. "The Germans, maybe even our own neighbors, people we had trusted, they came into our apartments and homes after we were sent to the Vélodrome d'Hiver or any of the holding centers the Nazis placed Jews in France. When I returned to my apartment, the furniture was upside down and the upholstery torn. I feel my daughter," he said in a hushed voice, tears soaking his cheeks. "Not her face. I don't see her face. Just the feeling of her."

"But then I'll s-see . . . ," I stammered, angry now, pinching my legs hard because I wanted to hurt, hurt as much on the outside as I did on the inside. "I'll see the faces of the partisans, right down to the moles on their cheeks and necks. I can even see one of the partisans' cleft palate." I saw clearly the piercing, cold blue-green eyes, too, of the SS guard who had killed a man in front of me. Us HASAG workers had been en route to somewhere then. The train would stop every few hours or days, and we prisoners would all be ordered out to dig anti-tank ditches, trenches deep and wide enough to sink enemy vehicles. The man, Papa's age, had been assigned to work with me. He was sickening with cough. His eyes had turned doughy, the whites yellowing. He was sick and he knew it, for he just threw down his shovel. "Good luck, son," he said. "You're on your own."

Jews who abandoned their work knew their fates. If they were being watched by a kind guard, they'd be shouted at once to return to work. But most of the guards, they were brutal. The Jewish man, who might have been a rabbi, a butcher, a storyteller, a grandfather, maybe all these things, was shot right in front of me—a bullet to his head and another aimed at his heart. I watched his body crumple to the ground, his face twisting and contorting, until it sank and turned to slate, his eyes open, staring, unblinking and hollow.

Regaining my senses, I began to shovel fast and hard, knowing well enough by now that for every Jew who defied the Germans like this, they'd sometimes go wild and shoot at least one more so those still alive would get the message to follow orders.

I felt the barrel of a soldier's gun at the back of my head. An SS man moved in close and whispered for me to follow him. I walked, urinating on myself from fear, down the line of Jews digging trenches. No one looked up, all shifting their eyes to the ground, fearing, like they should, that once I was dead, the guard might come for one of them next.

When we were out of sight, the SS man ordered me to stop. He bent down and pulled from a rucksack on the ground an apple. He handed it to me and smiled. "I remember every detail of this man's face—the high cheekbones, the wisps of straw-blond hair that fell out beneath his helmet, his perfect white teeth. He was Chaim's age," I told the professor now. "But I can't see my mama or my brothers anymore, Golda, or Nathan . . . or Papa, even Chaim."

I stared off then at nothing, my insides churning, my heart beating so fast, I was worried it would stop, wanting to weep and hit and lash out all at the same time. "The only thing I remember is hatred," I whispered softly. "There is no God. If there was, God would make me remember love."

The professor and I sat quietly, watching a hummingbird dance among flowers.

"Sometimes I wonder if I even had a life before the death camps," I finally said in a low voice. "When I do remember fragments of my life before . . . it's like these are dreams and they never happened."

"I feel that way, too," the professor said after a long pause. "I think we all do. But I know my daughter—I know she was real. Because I see her in you."

16

"We each decide whether to make ourselves learned or ignorant, compassionate or cruel, generous or miserly. No one forces us. No one decides for us, no one drags us along one path or the other. We are responsible for what we are."

—*Moses Maimonides (adapted)*

MY BROTHER MOTEL *and I stood side by side, craning our necks to peer out the tiny front window of our home, pushing aside Mama's lace curtains.*

For days, we had been hearing the airplanes of the German Luftwaffe flying overhead, the blast of distant dropping bombs. The bigger cities were targets. In Skarżysko-Kamienna, Chaim told us we were safe because of the munitions factory. The Germans dared not bomb something they wanted for their own.

When the bombs had died down, German tanks and trucks

rumbled along our street, shaking the houses. They were fol-
lowed by soldiers on motorcycles, then soldiers on horses,
and then foot soldiers wearing pointy helmets.

I wanted to be outside, to stand off to the side and wave to
the German Army. In each of my hands, I gripped one of my
wooden toy soldiers that Chaim and Papa had carved. They
had built me entire armies from slabs of oak. I wanted to
show the German military men, show them I would one day
be just like them, a soldier, too. I wanted to tell the Germans
that I enacted great battles using stones, twigs, and leaves to
build my fortresses. I even dug with my fingers tiny trenches.
The German Army men would surely be impressed that
Chaim had taught me battle techniques and shared his train-
ing schedule with the Polish Land Forces, like how to go for
days with little food, eating at certain times to conserve and
preserve energy, just like in real battles when the army might
be stuck in the forests for days. I knew what roots, leaves,
grasses, and flowers were edible and which were poison so I
could stay in battle-ready position for a long time if I needed
to. Chaim taught me how to attack by stealth, not by might.

But when the Germans came to Skarżysko-Kamienna,
Mama told me and Motel we had to stay inside. It was dan-
gerous out on the road. The tanks might not see us, especially
me, she said. I was little, after all. There was something she
was not telling me.

When the Germans came, that's when Mama's hands
started to shake, her back started to curve, and her hair
became brittle and coarse like she was aging a year for each
day. The Germans immediately took over the government
buildings, hoisting their bloodred swastika flags, telling us

all that they were now our bosses. Posters were plastered throughout the town, Chaim told Mama one night, saying Jews were criminals. Jewish-owned shops were boarded up with JUDE *painted in large letters blazoned across the front. Jews were not allowed to walk on the sidewalks, were not allowed to leave their homes past a certain time each night, were not allowed to shop at certain stores, were not allowed to use the parks, including the pathways twisting along the Kamienna River.*

Not long after the Germans came, two soldiers knocked on our door. They asked if Mama could make them tea. The two men, each the size of Chaim and not much older than him, too, sat at Papa's big table. Mama asked them, in a faltering voice, if they'd like to put some Kiddush wine in their tea. "It's very tasty," she said. "Sweet. Very good."

The soldiers loved Mama's tea and had some of her honey pastries afterward.

When the men left, Papa exhaled and told me, "See, these Germans are civilized people. They do not want to hurt us."

A few days later, more soldiers came. Their uniforms weren't all the same—some had different markings, different colors, and each represented different brutalities.

The SS, who wore pipe-blue uniforms, were the worst of all.

When they came to Skarżysko-Kamienna, that's when the shootings started.

At first, I didn't know what the sounds were, like firecrackers exploding in the air. I wondered if it was a celebration and we were missing it. I jumped up and down, begging Mama to let me go outside and see.

Mama, who was fading now, shrinking into herself, told me no. I wasn't even allowed to go to the outhouse without one of my older brothers accompanying me.

The Germans killed the mayor of Skarżysko-Kamienna. The Germans banned Jewish religious services. The Germans sent Jewish mamas and papas, anyone of working age, to farm or to work in the factories they took over and gave to German-owned companies.

Across Poland, lawyers, doctors, professors, artists, musicians, journalists, politicians, and businessmen were murdered. I overheard Chaim tell Papa the Germans killed the educated, anyone who could lead resistance movements or movements to rise up against the Nazis. Chaim said the Nazis wanted Poland as part of their plan for "Lebensraum," or living space, which meant eventually the entire country would be farmland, farmland for Germans to live on and expand their population.

Chaim said that the Polish Land Force, the Polish Army, those who hadn't been killed during the German invasion had fled—some into Russia, where he hoped to go, others west to join up with Allied forces. Polish Air Force officers were heading to England to join the British Royal Air Force. Chaim said there was an agreement between France, Great Britain, and Poland. If Germany invaded Poland, the French and British would come to our aid. But Chaim said no one was coming. Poland had been abandoned by her allies. We were on our own.

Mama gave us all armbands that she'd sewn and that the Germans said Jews had to wear: the armbands were black and white with a yellow Star of David. I was nine, the exact age children had to start wearing the armband that told the armies watching us that we were Jewish.

Chaim had advance warning that we were going to be evacuated from our house. So when a German soldier came and told us we had to move to a place called the Jewish Quarter, or the ghetto, Mama had already packed our things and Papa had loaded up the push wagon with our blankets and mattresses, suitcases and framed photographs of our family.

We walked on cobblestone streets, red from the blood of people shot. Papa mumbled the entire way that this was all a mistake. Bad men among good.

"This will be over soon," he kept repeating. "The Germans are civilized people. Look at their composers, Johann Sebastian Bach and Ludwig van Beethoven, artists like Hans Holbein and writers like Johann Wolfgang von Goethe."

Goethe was from Frankfurt. Buchenwald, which means "beech forest," was located, Jakow later told me, near the oak trees where Goethe would sit and write. On the main gate to the camp was written "Jedem das Seine" (to each his own), which Jakow said meant that the Germans could do anything they wanted because they considered themselves the master race.

I wanted to shout that at Papa. "Look! Look . . . at what your civilized people did!"

———

I started to write my story, starting with my time with the partisans.

When Papa learned I had snuck my way back into the

HASAG barracks, running away from the partisans, he did not greet me with love and kindness. He didn't act like he missed me. Instead, like when I'd run away from the Brankowski farm, he beat me. He laid me over his lap and smacked my bottom.

I was so confused.

I didn't know what he wanted from me.

I wanted him to remember when he would slip złoty in my pocket to buy ice cream, fudge, or peppermint sticks at the candy store or sit me on his lap when he talked to the elders or told stories. Since the ghetto, it was like he was trying to cut me out of him, out of us, the family, and every part of me bled. I thought I was good until the Nazis told me I was bad. And Papa, I felt, he believed them.

That's what I wrote first.

The professor said where we start our stories tells a lot about what we're really feeling, even if we don't know it ourselves, like our unconscious was trying to speak to us. The professor asked me if I was angry with Papa.

I didn't want that conversation, so I ripped up the pages of my notebook and started over.

I wrote about Yom Kippur 1942. In the afternoon of the eve of Hoshanah Rabbah, I snuck out of our ghetto apartment, darting past Mama, who was bathing Nathan in the metal tub she would bathe me in. I wanted to see what was happening outside. I hadn't left our ghetto apartment since Abram and I were chased by the Jewish police and we had to jump into the Kamienna River to save ourselves. On that night, I got another beating from Papa and Mama who, with crying eyes, begged me to never go outside again except for *cheder*, which was held in the basement of the apartment building next door to us.

Around me, death breathed, like the angel Azrael was walking among us. Street urchins with torn and dirty clothes and faces stretched out blackened hands, begging for a crust of bread. The soup kitchens were dry and had to close up early every day. Those who had been fed were fighting with the hungry, who were demanding scraps. On the streets lay men, old women, and young children dead from famine with newspaper placed over their faces as a sign of respect, since we could not follow Jewish customs for how to bury them.

I arrived at the main square just as a number of peasant carts pulled up. A woman close to me mumbled that the carts had come from Shidlovze. The Jews in the carts were naked. I turned my eyes away as the guards divided them into two lines, sending one group toward HASAG, the other toward the train station. I watched as the guards beat the people in the second line, pulling their hair, whipping them with pistols.

I stopped then and remembered something. Mama had told me when I was little to always find the best of people, something good in everyone I met. I was a horrible person because I couldn't find anything good about these guards, the Nazis, the soldiers from other countries who worked with them.

I ended up ripping these pages, too.

———

One late morning, when the professor and I had decided to take a break for the afternoon and head into Paris to listen to army men performing jazz, there was a note tacked to my dorm room door, saying Madame Minc wanted to see me.

I felt dread moving through me. Someone was dead. I was about to receive the news.

I gripped the banister hard, unsure I was even walking. I felt I was floating as I moved toward the office. When I opened the door, I stared into the round, smiling face of a woman with coiffed blond hair. I exhaled. Madame Minc would not be delivering bad news with guests around. I had been summoned for another reason. I quickly pulled myself together and stood straight, shoulders back, head up, the way I would at roll call at HASAG and then Buchenwald. I don't know why. I guess I just sensed from the way she carried herself that this woman was important.

The woman's smile was warm and inviting, and I relaxed some more. Her arm moved gracefully through the air until it pointed to a chair set beside a man, equally as well dressed as she.

"This is Jane Renaud-Brandt and her husband, Jean," Madame Minc started. "She's a benefactor of the OSE." I didn't know what a benefactor was, so I just nodded, making a mental note to ask the professor. One thing I'd learned very early on at HASAG was to listen and nod, agree to everything, even if the orders were barked out in a language I didn't understand. Disagreeing, asking questions, got people killed.

The woman's musky perfume filled the room. I stifled a cough.

"Hello," Jane said, motioning for me to take the seat beside her. I realized then that I was still standing.

"Hello," I whispered back, sitting down slowly.

"You seem sad?" Jane asked.

I shrugged.

"I've heard about you, Romek," Jane continued. "You are studying French, and I understand it is very good now."

I shrugged again.

"Your family was from Poland?"

I nodded slowly.

"I have two sons your age and a daughter a little younger. They would like to meet you. Would you like to come to my home sometime?"

I looked up and saw her staring at me. "Me?" I asked, surprised.

Jane nodded.

"But I'm dirty, and I—I am not so sure they would like me," I stammered. Like when I had met Aurore, I was self-conscious again about my appearance, who I was, what I had been through. How could I even begin to talk to someone who hadn't been through what I had?

"I came before," Jane continued. "You didn't see me. But I saw you. The others were playing football, but you stood off to the side looking so sad, like you do now. Maybe Jean and I can help you be happy a bit."

"We're all sad," I whispered, looking down again, this time at my scuffed shoes. "Just some of us are better at hiding it."

"I wanted to get to know you then, because I thought you are a very smart boy," Jane said, as if she hadn't heard me.

I opened my mouth to tell her that the other boys from Buchenwald were taking high school math and science courses and some were already enrolled in French schools.

I wasn't smart at all. But as the words were about to tumble out, I glanced over at Madame Minc, who shook her head like she knew what I was about to say.

"I'd like you to come to my house one weekend," Jane pressed on. "I can take you to the opera and the symphony. Have you ever been?"

"Only what I have heard at Écouis and here," I mumbled. But I thought back to Papa and the Beethoven he loved to listen to. How his favorite piece, "Sonata No. 14" or the "Moonlight Sonata," would fill our home, moving like mist out under the door and through the tiny cracks in the walls so that the music could even be heard on the street.

"And to some of my favorite restaurants," Jane was saying.

"I don't know," I said, shaking my head slowly. I was scared, very afraid. I was just starting, taking very baby steps, to feel comfortable talking to Aurore, the only person not a Buchenwald Boy or brought in to help us Buchenwald Boys. What would I say to Jane's children? What could we talk about? What would Jane think of me when no matter what she did, I wouldn't be happy, not ever again?

Madame Minc cleared her throat. "Can you try, Romek? Just one weekend. If you don't want to go back, you don't have to."

"Madame thinks you might really like coming to our apartment, experiencing French culture," Jane picked up. "I hear you like to go to the jazz clubs. You know, jazz was introduced to Paris during the first World War. Jazz, when the Germans occupied France, was our quiet, Parisian way of opposing Nazi oppression. The Nazis with their straight

184

lines, order, punctuality, and purity of race were the complete opposite of jazz, which infuses music traditions from around the world and is free and wild and improvised. I heard you feel something for jazz. That it calls to you the way it does to the French. I'd like to take you to more concerts, maybe see Josephine Baker. Édith Piaf, too. She is not so much jazz, but she is a friend of mine."

Jean cleared his throat, startling me because I had forgotten he was in the room. He dug out of his breast pocket a chocolate bar and passed it to me.

I stared at the glittery wrapping.

"There are good people in this world, Romek," Jakow had told me as he wrapped around me a sweater large enough to fit the biggest man at Buchenwald. It was winter and even still, some man, another freezing prisoner, had given his sweater from the Red Cross to me to keep me warm. "Where there are monsters," Jakow had said, "there are also angels taking our hands. Don't ever forget that."

I found myself agreeing to Jane's proposal.

———

After Jane and Jean left, Madame Minc talked to me about how the OSE was also pairing us Buchenwald Boys with French Jewish boys living in Paris.

She said the French boys would help us feel more part of the society and culture. She wanted to pair me with a boy named Jacques, who had a younger brother, Henri. As Madame Minc spoke about how the French Jewish boys could teach us teen culture, do things teenage boys were doing, my mind drifted back to when I was imprisoned in

185

Częstochowa. One dawn, just before heading outside for roll call, I'd looked out the dusty window of the barracks and seen a boy in the distance, walking in the adjacent field. He was maybe my age, and he was swinging a metal bucket. I watched him pull water from the well and then move back across the field, toward a house with smoke rising like fading ink from a chimney. I wondered then what his life was like. Was he having breakfast with his family? Did he even know there were boys his age trapped on the other side of the barbed wire fence, watching him? Was he going to school? He was wearing a red wool scarf that his mother or grandmother had probably knit for him.

A red scarf. I remembered then vowing that when I made it home, I would have Mama knit me a red wool scarf.

"Romek, I don't want you to get your hopes up," I caught Madame Minc saying.

"What?" I asked, not sure what she was talking about.

"Were you even listening to me?"

I shook my head.

"Romek, there is a boy in Switzerland . . . a boy who may be your brother Motel."

Jacques and Henri.

17

JACQUES AND HENRI reminded me for some strange reason of my brothers Motel and Moishe.

Moishe hadn't wanted to be a tailor like Papa. He also hadn't wanted to be a soldier like Chaim. Moishe didn't even seem to want to be a kid. While Motel and I would play football, catch frogs, or just run outside, Moishe would twist wires together and fix broken electronics for neighbors. He wanted to go to university for engineering and knew to be admitted as a Jew, he would have to be among the best at school, because Poland allotted Jews only a few placements in every program. Moishe spent all his free hours studying and was not just among the best, but he had the top marks in his school and all the surrounding schools, too, all the way to Warsaw. That autumn, when the Nazis invaded Poland, Moishe was set to apply to university. Then the Nazis imposed new rules, one of which was that Jews couldn't go to university. Motel and Moishe, who were close in age, drew closer then. Motel told Moishe that he would help him get into university any way he could.

Jacques and Henri talked about the brass bands in the park they'd like to take me to and the dances at the public halls. Jacques and Henri were both taller than I was. They chatted, were friendly and open, but weren't know-it-alls like Salek. I felt they genuinely wanted to get to know me.

Jacques and Henri took turns telling me that their papa had placed them in a Christian monastery during the Nazi occupation of France. The boys had to pretend to learn how to be monks. Their mama also went into hiding in a village in the south. But their papa was missing, and a friend of the family who had survived said she thought she'd seen him at Auschwitz being sent to nearby Birkenau, which almost always meant death.

There was something about these two boys that when they talked seemed familiar. As the path twisted beside a narrow river, I felt for a moment like I was walking with two of my brothers. That gave me a shiver, for I hadn't felt that with Salek, Marek, or even Abe.

In Paris, the boys were telling me, if someone showed ID cards that said they were Jewish, they could get into movies for free. Jacques and Henri had identification cards saying they were Jewish. I told them I had the war-veteran pin that allowed me to get into theaters and concerts for free. The boys had recently seen *Madame Pimpernel* or *Paris Underground*, as well as *Assignment: Paris!* They liked movies about the war, they said, because they hadn't had a lot of information in the monastery and hadn't known what was going on. Unlike me, they wanted to know what happened to Europe and how it happened and could it happen again? Jacques then started to talk about a new Tarzan movie being released. My ears picked up. As Jacques climbed on a metal gate, thumped his chest, and then called out like Tarzan, I surprised myself by asking them if we could go to see the Tarzan film together.

As we were making our way back to the center, me walking in the middle of the two of them, Aurore rounded a corner and headed directly for us. I felt butterflies in my stomach and was sure I had stopped breathing. She was with two friends, all the girls dressed in matching school uniforms. As Aurore neared, I could see her face flush. Her eyes met mine and seemed to light up.

Our passing did not go unnoticed. When the girls were out of earshot, Jacques and Henri teased me that I had a girlfriend. I waved them off, saying no one would like me. Aurore was just a friend. She was teaching me about bees. But the boys didn't accept my answer. They said they would teach me how to swing dance so I could ask her out.

"You could do with some more fashionable clothes, too," Henri said, stopping to study me.

"Your pants are too big and your shirt is too small," Jacques said. "But that's easy to fix. You have a nice face, nice eyes. You look fit. Why do you think a girl wouldn't like you?"

"Look closer at my scars," I told them. I then proceeded to tell them the story of how I had been burned.

They both cooed that the scars were barely noticeable. "It just makes your skin look darker in spots," added Henri. "Besides. Girls don't want cookie cutters. The scars make you unique and handsome like the French actors Lucien Baroux, Jean Marais, and Fernandel."

"You stand out in that pure and honest sort of way like the actor Raimu."

"Like you're the boy next door, who every girl trusts," Jacques chimed in.

I nearly choked from the description, how Jacques and Henri saw me. I felt anything but pure and honest.

Besides, I knew enough that I'd lost a lot of years when I was supposed to grow into liking girls the way Chaim liked Golda. My last friendship with a girl was Halinka, and that hadn't turned out so well. I didn't know how to talk to girls, let alone what to do around them, even though at the mansion there were a few French Jewish orphan girls, sisters to their brothers who lived in the building. When I saw them, I perspired and felt flushed and just moved away.

"We'll bring you home with us," Jacques said. "You can meet our *maman*. Maybe you can take some of our clothes that don't fit anymore."

I thought of Mama then and how she would take Motel's and Moishe's clothes when they outgrew them. She would mend the holes, seal the seams that had stretched, and put on new buttons. After a good wash and press, my brothers' clothes became my new clothes.

Henri asked me what music I liked. I said I didn't really know music, except for jazz and Papa's Beethoven. They liked the French singers, including Charles Trenet. When they mentioned Édith Piaf's name, I told them about Jane. They recognized Jane's surname, saying if this was the Jane they knew from society sections of the newspapers, her family had founded a company that made washing machines and munitions. Her father, Jacques told me, had invented the bazooka gun.

But I didn't feel like talking anymore, thinking back to HASAG, wondering if maybe that was why Jane wanted to meet me, to have me go to work in one of her factories. Maybe going to her apartment was a trick, the way the Nazis would be nice one minute and then shoot someone the next.

"Romek, we'll help you," Henri called over his shoulder as they left me at the mansion. "We'll help you with Aurore."

But I wasn't thinking of Aurore. I was trying to figure out ways to get out of going to Jane's apartment.

———

I became a thorn in Madame Minc's side.

Several times a day, I would sit, drumming my fingers on the ground and tapping a nervous foot, waiting outside her office. I would spend what seemed like hours pacing the long hallway so much that I could see marks where I had worn some of the carpet away.

Every time I saw Madame Minc, she would sigh and say no news.

Madame Minc reminded me that Motel lived in Switzerland, a country away. She had to send letters to the OSE staff person there, who had to then confirm Motel's identity by cross-checking his story with mine. Apparently, Switzerland wasn't going to allow the older boys entry. But Rabbi Shachter was adamant that they, too, needed the opportunity to heal. Some of the older boys also had younger brothers who were given visas for Switzerland, and he didn't want siblings separated, so he had forged birth dates, making the older boys younger. Then Switzerland had to send this information by post back to us. We could be waiting weeks, Madame Minc said, so she encouraged me to find something to do to distract myself during this time.

Henri and Jacques invited me for Friday Shabbat dinner. At first I hesitated at the invitation, letting them know that I wasn't religious. But they assured me that the dinner would be casual, just about getting together. Besides, Henri told me, his *maman* had a friend she'd met while in hiding, a Polish Jewish woman, she wanted me to meet.

The boys lived in a one-story house in Champagne, east of Paris. Paint peeled on the outside of their building, and wood was chipped in places.

When Henri pushed open the front door to the house, I stopped dead in my tracks, though, as I inhaled the rich aromas of frying garlic, onion, and chicken with a mix of herbs, including rosemary, that Mama would use in her chicken soup. Even the smell of the interior, musty wood mixed with wildflowers, reminded me of home.

Jacques walked up behind me and clapped me gently on the back. "You okay?"

Not realizing I had been holding my breath, I let out a long sigh and then cleared my throat. "I . . . I . . . I just, I . . . ," I stammered. Before I could finish, a woman with her hair tied up in a loose bun and wearing an apron over a skirt and blouse came barreling toward me. Her arms were stretched out. When she was near enough, she whisked me into a big hug. "Welcome, welcome, welcome," she said over and over again in Yiddish.

When she pulled away, she said her name was Rose. She was Henri and Jacques's mother.

In the living room, which contained a well-worn blue sofa

and two matching chairs, Henri introduced me to Hannah. Hannah was much older than I'd expected. A grandmother for certain. She spoke to me in Polish, asking where I was from. I was just about to answer when Rose called out for Hannah, saying she needed help. Rose was starting to set the table. I looked over at the table and gasped. It was just like ours in Skarżysko-Kamienna.

As the women prepared the table for Shabbat, lighting candles and setting out cups for the Kiddush wine, Henri, Jacques, and I spread out on the floor and played a game of jacks.

When Rose put the steaming bowl of chicken soup on the table, she apologized that there wasn't a lot of meat available in France for most people. "It's mostly broth and carrots and some wild mushrooms I picked from the garden," Rose said. "But I added some sprigs of rosemary and black pepper for flavor."

"That's how my mama would make our soup sometimes," I said, not thinking.

Hannah was bringing out a pot of steaming boiled potatoes when she asked me again where I was from.

"Poland," I said. I was focused on our game. I had the most jacks and was determined to win.

"I know that," she replied with a laugh. "But where in Poland?"

"A small city. You wouldn't know it," I said over my shoulder. Then, remembering to be polite, I added, "Where do you come from, Rose?"

"Russia," she said, poking her head out from the kitchen.

"What city are you from?" Hannah asked, probing. She

195

wasn't going to let this go. "You may be surprised. I might know it."

I thrust my arms in the air after sweeping up the last remaining jacks. "Skarżysko-Kamienna," I said, turning to address Hannah properly.

I heard Rose let out a little yell. I looked over at her. She was carrying a stack of dinner plates. Her eyes were wide as saucers, and her face had turned white.

"I have a brother in Skarżysko," she said slowly, her voice shaking. "What did your father do? Wh-what . . . ," she added, stammering, "what . . . is his name?"

"He was a tailor . . . and a haberdasher," I replied, standing up, unsure what was going on.

"My brother made my table," Rose said, her entire body shaking.

Now my eyes grew wide. "Papa's name was Chil," I said, my voice tilting, as a sense of knowing floated over me, the way it had before Abe was able to get out that he was leaving. Rose dropped the dishes, and her body crumpled to the floor alongside them. I fought the urge to fall with her.

Henri and Jacques scurried to their mama's side, while I remained frozen to the spot.

"I had a feeling," said Hannah smugly. "I sense things sometimes, like I can tell fortunes. I'll read yours sometime."

I knew then why Jacques and Henri seemed so familiar. I didn't need Rose or Hannah to tell me.

"*Maman*, wake up!" Henri screamed, while Jacques shouted at Hannah to find a doctor.

Hannah laughed and said there was no need. "Rose has just had a shock. She'll be all right in a minute," she said.

Jacques ran to get some water. When he returned, Rose's eyelids were fluttering. "I just fainted," she said in a hushed voice.

As she pulled herself up, her cheeks red and glowing, tugging on her shirt at the same time to open the buttons and cool herself off, her eyes remained glued to me.

"What is it, *Maman*?" Jacques said, looking first at his mother, then at me. "Do you know Romek?"

"Yes," Rose finally said. "Yes. He's my nephew," she whispered. "Romek is your cousin. Romek . . . ," she said, trying to stand on swaying legs. Jacques and Henri guided their mother to the sofa.

"Chil is my brother. Romek," she repeated, "Romek, he is my flesh and blood."

18

I REMEMBERED NOW.

I remembered Rose.

I was a small child, maybe three or four. She had come to visit Papa. She stayed in our house. Mama and Papa gave her their bed, while Mama slept with Leah and Papa with Chaim and Abram.

Rose looked out of place in her wool suits and silk blouses, her pearls and white gloves. Most of the mamas in Skarżysko-Kamienna wore skirts so long, the tails swept the floor, with bulky shirts and sweaters. Most Polish Jewish mamas in Skarżysko-Kamienna wore headscarves, too, not hats like Rose with feathers and mesh. Their hair underneath was usually long, braided or tied back into some kind of bun. But Rose, she had hair that fell in curves down to her shoulders that she curled with her fingers. Rose wore blush and lipstick, too. I now remembered thinking that next to Golda, she was the most beautiful woman I had ever seen.

Rose was thinner now.

But then, we all were.

"I would never have recognized you," Rose said, gripping my hand. I swallowed hard. Of course she wouldn't recognize me. I didn't recognize myself.

Rose laughed then, and I remembered that laugh that had filled our home in Skarżysko-Kamienna. When Papa left Russia, escaping the pogroms, his sister was just a small child. When she was old enough, she married and, with her husband, moved to France. She never lived in Skarżysko-Kamienna.

Rose, I remembered then, had been dancing light. Now she seemed weighted down, full of worry, despite her giggles.

Henri and Jacques sat cross-legged on the floor, listening as their *maman* told stories of my papa, of their childhoods in Russia, of the cold winters, of sledding down hills on carved pieces of wood, of sharing each other's shoes because there wasn't enough money for the family to afford a pair for every child.

To my cousins, the storytelling seemed to be great fun. They begged for more and more, their faces alight.

To me and, I sensed, to Rose, too, it was more.

We each had found something to hang on to.

———

I told Rose, Henri, and Jacques what I could remember of my life . . . *my life before*, omitting, of course, the anger that had been brewing inside me toward Papa.

Memories were returning almost like a dam had broken.

It wasn't merely in my dreams but a scent, just as Leah

200

had said it would be. Rose's herbs that Mama had used in her cooking, too, or the taste of the sweet nectar of an apple, even the hum of an airplane overhead, and all of a sudden I was transported back in time. I told Rose and then the professor that it wasn't like I had forgotten these things. It was like I had put them somewhere, locked them away.

Nearly a year and a half after liberation, it was now like my brain was unfolding in front of me. And along with it came a fury that frightened me.

After several weeks had passed and still no news from Switzerland, after my usual schedule of studying, followed by trying to catch a glimpse of Aurore, and then more studying, interspersed with eating, I just couldn't take it anymore. I awoke with pounding headaches, and my entire body shook. I was sure I was slipping back into that trance I first had after learning I was unable to return to Poland. Papa, I thought one morning, was to blame for all of this.

And then the news I had been waiting for arrived.

The boy in Switzerland was not Motel. It was a boy named Mosze Waichmann.

Whatever I had been pushing down inside me, I couldn't hold back anymore. I wanted to punch someone, something. As Madame Minc talked in a soothing voice about how she would keep looking, she would leave no stone unturned to find any other surviving family, I chewed the inside of my mouth.

That night, I couldn't eat, couldn't sleep.

I tossed and turned.

In the morning, when I heard the swallows waking outside, I grabbed the rucksack Ralph had given me. I packed my toothbrush, my underwear, a change of clothes, and the shirt Abe had given me. I was leaving.

I could no longer hold back the urge to go in search of my family on my own.

———

I left some room in the rucksack for food. I was jamming breads, cheeses, fruits, canned peaches, and nuts into my pockets and backpack when the professor found me.

He was on his way into the mansion through the back kitchen door. He was carrying a stack of papers. He spied my army duffel bag with suspicion. "Going somewhere?" he asked, cocking an eyebrow.

I sank.

"You're writing your exam today, Romek," the professor said, motioning with his chin to the papers in his arms. "The test to see where you will place in school. Remember? You're ready for this. I know you are. I bet you'll be able to start high school in a few weeks!"

I swallowed hard. "I—I . . . ," I stammered. I had forgotten all about the test. I hadn't studied the night before.

I didn't know what to tell him. For nearly a year, this man had become like a big brother to me. He talked to me like I belonged in this world. But one thing I'd learned in the camps was that one day a friend, the next day an enemy. To survive, a person couldn't wait for anyone. If something felt off, not right, instinctual, like an animal, I went with that gut feeling. Now my gut was telling me to just leave. Or was it?

"Romek, whatever you think you're doing, don't. Write the exam," he pressed on. "Do you trust me?"

"I don't know what trust means anymore," I whispered. And I didn't. I was sinking again, second-guessing my own decision.

Boys started to rush past us on their way to breakfast. I took some of the professor's papers to lighten his load.

"Let's eat together," the professor said in a kind voice. "Have a coffee. Then write your exam. You can decide tomorrow what you want to do. We will do this together. You're not alone anymore," he added, putting a free hand on my shoulder.

I labored through the exam, which involved basic reading in French. It should have been easy. I was well versed in the *passé composé* and the other tenses. I was reading mystery chapter books now and French philosophy, including Voltaire. The literature component of the exam was the equivalent of picture books. The math was easy, or it should have been. Even the math problems, which I had practiced in various ways hundreds of times, I stumbled on. My eyes blurred, and I couldn't see the numbers straight.

All I thought of was Motel, how much I had wanted to believe that the boy in Switzerland was him. Papa had once said to me, "Trust in God, be patient, and never lose hope. That is life."

I had no hope anymore. But then, why should I? Papa had lost it first. I had learned losing my faith from him, hadn't I?

Beside me on the floor sat that duffel bag. I stared at it for the last fifteen minutes of the exam.

The professor was right. I couldn't leave the mansion.

Leah had written me from Palestine. It was very difficult there. She and Abram had little to no money and toiled all day long in the fields. There were days, she wrote, where they had the same amount of food to eat as they got when in the camps.

Poland, I couldn't go back there. A Polish family most likely had taken over my house. Poland was now under Soviet Union occupation. The Soviets didn't have concentration camps, but they weren't nice to the Jews, either. During the war, when they were in control of Eastern Poland, those who refused Soviet citizenship and Jews were sent to work on beet farms deep in Soviet Russia. Some Jews, I'd heard, were even sent to Siberia.

Ralph had disappeared, so I couldn't go to Russia or Eastern Europe with him and join up with the Communists. Knowing my luck, if I went alone, I'd end up with another wannabe band of Communists like the partisans. I had no way of knowing how to join a Communist movement.

I had nowhere to go, no one to help me look for my family, except for the people with the OSE.

That afternoon, I sat on the ledge by the black wrought-iron fence that lined Aurore's house, waiting for her to return from school. When she approached, I told her that I needed to go away for a while—not away as in physically, but I had to spend some time focusing on me. I told her I knew I had failed the exam to enter high school. I told her I had an anger inside me, a pain, and I was throwing my life away until I sorted it out. I didn't want to drag her down with me. I was going to refocus everything on my studies and getting into school and dealing with the deep pit of sorrow that threatened to swallow me like the whale did Jonah.

I hoped Aurore would understand; I wanted her to find someone else.

"I'm not good enough for you. I can't give you what you want and need. I am not in a good place," I told her.

"When you're in a good place, will you find me?" she asked, looking at me with those startling green-blue eyes.

I melted. "Of course," I said, shaking my head, "but, Aurore, I may never be in a great place. If you meet some other boy and like him, please do not think of me. Go. I will be happy for you."

Jane Renaud-Brandt.

19

FOR WEEKS, I put off going to Jane's apartment.

I told Madame Minc I felt sick. Gripping my stomach, I moaned.

Another time, I said I had too much studying. And I did! I had missed the September start date to attend regular high school, but the professor said I had to go to school anyway. Elementary school. I was in a classroom with ten-year-olds, ten-year-olds who spoke faster and better French than I did and who whispered in quiet voices that I was stupid, slow, an imbecile. Little did they know. "I'm a spy," I hissed at them one day. "I hear everything you are saying." That shut them up, because despite the fact that the Nazis had been gone for nearly two years, even the children remembered what it was like to live under occupation: afraid the man in the room was a spy sending information to the Germans on who was bad and who was good. In fact, I thought after, I would make a great spy, and I put that on my list to tell the professor of potential jobs I could do. Most of all, I was determined to get out of the class with the kids and into a classroom with teens my age by January. I was studying day and night—algebra, math problems, reading French classics like Alexandre Dumas's *The Count of Monte Cristo* and Albert Camus's *The Outsider*.

Eventually, though, Madame Minc guessed enough that I was stalling on the Jane topic and so I told her why. I was afraid Jane was sending me to work in her munitions factory. Madame Minc tilted her head back and laughed, the curls bobbing up and down on her head as she did so, her chest heaving like I was part of a comedy show. I was angry at first, telling her to stop, that she didn't understand how for more than two years, all I did was work in a munitions factory, twelve hours a day, six days a week, making arms that the Germans used to kill Jews. Madame Minc quickly composed herself and apologized. Her expression turned serious. But then I started laughing. Hearing myself speak my fears, I realized how funny and irrational they actually were. Madame Minc assured me that Jane had no intention of having me work in any of her factories.

I never saw the inside of the Château de Ferrières.

But if I had, I suspected it would look a lot like Jane's apartment.

Located on Avenue Montaigne in the 8th *arrondissement*, the apartment sprawled several floors and was like a mansion within a larger building. The various floors were connected by winding staircases, the banisters of which looked like they were jeweled in gold. There was also an elevator for when Jane or Jean or one of their children was tired, which took them up to their bedrooms.

The wallpaper in each of the rooms was made of silk.

Each room was a different color—robin's-egg blue, sunset rose, canary yellow. The furniture, I later learned, was from the Louis XV period, hundreds of years old and expensive, heirlooms, which meant passed down from Jane's papa to Jane. On the walls were what I discovered were very rare and priceless paintings, including a Pierre-Auguste Renoir. The lighting for the paintings was done by the same person who had done the lighting in the Louvre.

After introducing me to her family, her children Michel, Claude, and Isabelle, Jane took me to La Mère Catherine, the oldest bistro, she said, in Paris, founded in 1793. All the staff and many of the patrons knew Jane as she walked in, saying hello and asking about her day.

Jane and I sat at a table near the back. While I waited for eggs Benedict, Jane explained that during the German occupation of Paris, members of the Nazi Party would eat at the bistro. Many French businesses, she said in a conspiratorial voice, had to cater to the Nazis, but the French staff often worked for the resistance movements, passing on information about the conversations they overheard. I soon relaxed, realizing that Jane talked to me like the professor did, like I was a grown-up. I liked that, and I found myself soon telling Jane how embarrassed I was about my appearance and how I felt I didn't belong in the world anymore. Most of all, I was afraid to eat in public.

Jane was a doer, I discovered quickly enough. She asked the waiter for a seat in the back near the kitchen, whispering to me as I followed her to a new table that once I felt comfortable, we could return to her table. "But for now, in the back, no one will see us."

After our meal, she took me to the Galeries Lafayette on Boulevard Haussmann. In the men's department, Jane had me trying on tweed suits and crinkly cotton shirts. Even a tuxedo, she said, for when she took me to the opera. My first outing with Jane was just for the day. I played chess with her children, had an afternoon snack on Jane's terrace with Jean. I returned that evening to Le Vésinet with bags full of pants, shirts, sweaters, suspenders, even French berets and new underwear. I also had several boxes of meringues to hand out to the boys.

I spent many weekends with Jane and her family during the winter of 1947, eating pastries and sipping coffees rich with cream and sprinkled with chocolate and cinnamon. Her children accepted me like I was one of them. They didn't really like chess, they eventually told me, or the concertos they had mastered on the grand piano, which they performed for me. I told them I had just been learning the violin when the Germans invaded Poland. My older brothers could all play. They showed me their rooms that were bigger than my entire house back in Skarżysko-Kamienna and said they would much rather go to a Tarzan film than any of this cultured stuff their mother had them do. I laughed then and felt even more at home.

Jane and I made a deal that I could choose one activity for us to do, she the next. She took me with her children to see the Tarzan film several times that winter and invited Henri and Jacques to tag along. And to the opera, for which Claude made an excuse for him and his siblings, saying they had other plans. Jane had bought box seats at the Palais Garnier, overlooking the stage. We peered at the performers through tiny binoculars made with gold. We'd had singers come to

Écouis and the mansion at Le Vésinet, but none sang quite like those in the opera. The sopranos could reach such high notes and so piercingly, I was sure the crystal chandeliers shook with excitement, and the alto and baritone voices moved right through me, like a current taking me out to sea. Jane also took me to the Paris Opera Ballet.

I didn't mind the opera or ballet, but, like her children, I much preferred the western movies like those starring John Wayne. At first, I felt badly that I wasn't as cultured as perhaps some of the other Buchenwald Boys. I wondered if Jane wanted to trade me in for someone else who enjoyed the art galleries and symphonies. But over a catered dinner one night in her apartment, Claude told me that Jane just wanted to show me things I would never have experienced before. She didn't care whether I liked them or not. She just wanted to show me options. Then Michel winked and said he was happy it was me and not them being dragged around to all the stuffy cultural things their mother liked to do. "You're doing us a big favor." He grinned.

Jane and I often walked along the River Seine, crisscrossing across the bridges with the Eiffel Tower always in full view. We sometimes stopped to have seafood lunches on a barge with Jane's friends, who she told me after were famous actors, politicians, playwrights, and singers. They would get chatty and giggly on champagne and smoke cigars. Sometimes, when they were very tipsy, they performed monologues from plays Jane whispered to me were famous or songs that she said were played on the radio.

Every Friday, I tried to go to Shabbat with Rose, Henri, and Jacques. There I would learn more stories of Papa, including how he and Mama met. The *schadchen* had matched them, but Rose said it was love at first sight. "You know, in our tiny Eastern European shtetls, it was rare for a man and woman to love each other that much on their wedding day," she told me. "But Chil and Rifka were in love. Their love was eternal." Rose then teared, talking about her own husband who was missing, presumed dead. "It wasn't the same with us," she said, "but I grew to love him."

In January, I started high school, in a class with no one I knew, but now the kids didn't make fun of me.

For my sixteenth birthday on February 2, 1947, Jane took me to a restaurant called Maxim's de Paris, where I was introduced to pâté foie gras and caviar. I much preferred eggs Benedict and buttery or chocolate-dipped croissants and Jane, knowing me well by now, made sure I was also served a buttery pasta dish and, for dessert, chocolate pudding. I sipped champagne for the first time and ended the meal with a cheese platter, devouring the Camembert that I had grown to love. With Rose and my cousins, my birthday was spent singing Yiddish songs. Hannah made cabbage rolls, salted herring, and potato latkes to remind me of Poland and, for dessert, Polish cream cake.

Always when I left Jane, her driver would take me back to the mansion in La Vésinet past the Arc de Triomphe into the chestnut tree–lined boulevards of the suburbs. I had never been in a car before Jane's. No one owned cars in Skarżysko-Kamienna; at least the Jewish families didn't. Families visited relatives in other towns by horse and buggy. There were sleds for winter snows pulled by horses, too. When the cattle trains stopped and the Nazis ordered us prisoners off to dig anti-tank ditches, sometimes I would spy the German vehicles. These cars were sleek and long and flew the Nazi swastika flag. Chaim had a truck, but it wasn't his. It was for his work with HASAG. Hannah told me that Chaim likely had lied about his identity to HASAG. The German-owned company would never have allowed a Polish soldier to be a driver. "But we're Jewish," Hannah said. "We never leave family. We stay together always. The Nazis knew that. That's why they lied to Jews going to Treblinka and other death camps, saying to 'stay with your relatives. You will all work together.'"

By the spring of 1947, one could say I wanted for nothing. Salek, Joe, Marek, and I went to the movies and jazz clubs when we had time. They, too, had met mentors and people like Jane who were helping them integrate back into life. We were all studying: Salek and Joe had even been accepted to a vocational school for the autumn.

But never far from my thoughts was Papa and that anger that simmered inside me.

"Cry," Rose said to me on one of my visits. "Yell, scream, let it out, the pain. They may be all gone except for Leah." But I couldn't. I wasn't angry with the Nazis for what they did to us. I was angry that Papa could have left Poland before the Nazis came. Papa wasn't supposed to just tell me everything would be all right. Even when the Nazis came, Papa should have stayed with me. I was angry that he broke my trust.

––––––

I was back in my house in Skarżysko-Kamienna.

It was a midsummer night. I know, because Mama had opened the windows. A soft breeze blew her lace curtains,

213

and the windswept flames of the Shabbat candles cast mov-ing shadows on the walls.

Papa and the elders were there, flanked by Chaim and some of his Jewish friends from the army. Not everyone had seats. Some were standing, pacing.

There were visitors among them, too. Two men I hadn't seen before. They spoke Yiddish with an accent. "They're from Germany," Moishe whispered to me. "They come with news of what is happening there."

In Germany, Jews had great lives. They held positions of power in business, law, politics, theater, journalism, and medicine. "We're backward here compared to our cousins in Germany," Papa would say.

But the German Jews who sat around the table talked of something else—of their businesses destroyed, the burning of the Reichstag in Berlin that was blamed on Jews and which paved the way for Kristallnacht *in November 1938, also known as the Night of Broken Glass. On that night, the Ger-man SA troops destroyed all hope for Jews in Germany, the men were saying. They spoke of camps being built to imprison Adolf Hitler's political opponents, the Communists. These camps were also for Jews.*

Now the German Jews were fleeing—refugees, they called themselves—warning us to leave, too. The German Army would come to Poland next, the men said.

Chaim was set to go.

He begged Papa and the elders to depart, to get out of Poland.

"But the Germans are educated people," Papa said in a loud, booming voice, banging a fist on the table, shaking the wineglasses.

I had never seen Chaim so angry, pushing back his chair and glaring at Papa. His nostrils flared, and his face was red. I looked at his fists. He was squeezing them tight.

"I have a son," Chaim spat out. "I want Nathan to live. We have to leave, all of us, now." Chaim hissed at not just Papa but at the elders who were agreeing with Papa. "The Germans have already taken Austria and Czechoslovakia's Sudetenland. All of Czechoslovakia is next. No opposition. No friends coming to anyone's aid. Our army, my army, we can't hold the Germans back, and the Germans want to kill us Jews. Papa, I'm telling you." Chaim was now yelling. "The Germans aim to wipe out the Jews of Europe."

"No, they do not," Papa said, standing up now, facing Chaim. His face, too, was red and fuming.

Mama jumped in between them. "Chaim, dear Chaim," she whispered, rubbing his back. "Listen to your father. Always listen to him, like Nathan will do to you. We will leave but all together."

Three years later, at HASAG, in the gray, the sun seemingly covered in a perennial cloud, Papa started disappearing. It was not long after that Abram was killed. At first it was Papa's hair. It turned gray, and then, by the end of the week, white. His knees bent. His eyelids drooped.

"Papa, we are going to be all right, aren't we?" I asked him the last Sunday I saw him, before roll call, before selection. "Papa," I started screaming when he didn't answer. "Papa." I shook him, shook him hard, but his eyes just stared off at nothing. He had turned into one of the Muselmann workers, dead while still walking. It was like he didn't see me, didn't know me, didn't want me. It was like he wasn't there anymore.

An older man in the barracks moved toward me. He gently

spoke to me, saying Papa was just unwell, that he would be fine in a few days.

But he wasn't fine.

He disappeared that very day.

Gone.

———

"I believed him. I believed Papa's words that we would be all right, almost up until the very end," I told the professor one spring day. "Do you know what it is like to lose trust in the very person in whom you had placed all your faith? That's why I don't want to pray. I'm mad at Papa," I added in a hushed voice. "I am mad at God. When business was slow or when a storm came and damaged the house, even when we didn't have enough to eat in the ghetto, Papa would recite part of Psalm 91. He would say:

> *"He who dwells in the shelter of the Most High*
> *will rest in the shadow of the Almighty.*
> *I will say of the Lord, 'He is my refuge and my fortress,*
> *my God, in whom I trust.'"*

I lowered my head. "Papa was a fool," I said. "And we all believed him."

"Romek, you don't know this now, but you will in time. What the Nazis did was not God. And your father . . . *your father* didn't punish you when you returned from the Brankowskis' farm or from the partisans. He didn't abandon you. He wanted to save you," the professor said. "He would have died for you. He lives on in you."

———

One evening, nearing the longest day of the year, as Jane's driver was taking me back to the mansion, we detoured and pulled onto Aurore's street.

She was outside.

I asked the driver to stop, saying I would walk the rest of the way.

I stood and watched the car leave. Then, perspiring, my hands trembling from nerves, I moved toward Aurore. It had been more than eight months since I'd seen her; I wondered if she'd even know who I was anymore.

When she looked up, she waved.

"Hello," she said, smiling.

I cleared my throat. "How are the bees this evening?"

She laughed. "I'm actually looking at the flowers today," she said in a soft voice. "Come." She then motioned for me to follow her along a tiny rock path until we stopped near some rosebushes. "I planted these roses last spring," she said. "At night, they're so fragrant." She pointed to the white flowers. "When the moon is bright, it's like the white roses are dancing. And at night, they are the most fragrant of all the flowers."

She leaned in and inhaled. She then took my hand and indicated for me to do the same. She was right. The perfume of the roses was soft, delicate, warm, and peaceful.

"I live with my grandmother's sister, aunt, and uncle," she said. "We wanted something special to remember . . ." Aurore's voice trailed off then. I didn't need her to tell me. Her parents were gone, like Papa, like Chaim, like Motel, Moishe, Abram, Golda, and Mama. "My mama's favorite flower was the white rose."

We both sat down on a log, listening to twilight as it pulled its blanket over the top of us.

We must have sat there for half an hour, not saying a word, until my legs grew sore.

"*Maman* liked the moon, too," Aurore eventually said as the night sky drew out a crescent moon. "My father would always take us for walks after dinner, sometimes by the Seine, to watch the moon's rays caress the water. My mother used to say that the moon catches our dreams. I dream that *Maman* and Papa are watching over me."

"I like the night sky, too."

"I know. I saw you looking at it that night you lay down in my yard." We both laughed then. I hadn't realized that it was Aurore's garden.

"I need to go inside," she finally said. "I need to study. *Maman* wanted me to be a doctor or a teacher when I grew up. I want to do that for her. I have to live their dreams now, too."

"Do you want to go to a dance with me sometime?" I choked out, unsure myself from where the words had come.

She laughed again. She had a pretty laugh, reserved but genuine. "Yes," she murmured. "I would like that."

"I don't know how to dance," I wanted to tell her and take my invitation back. But I found myself smiling, too.

I followed her as she skipped off back down the path. Before she reached her door, though, she stopped, turned, and ran back toward me. She drew me in and kissed me softly on the cheek.

20

"MAMA," I BEGAN. "When are you going to die?"

"We'll talk about it later, Rachmilshu" she said, using my childhood nickname, which took my Yiddish name Rachmil and added "little one" at the end. Rachmilshu.

"I love you so much, so if you are going to die, then I want to die the day before you do," I said.

My house on Third of May Street appeared in front of me. I am not sure how old I was, but I do know it was Yom Kippur. Papa was very serious during Yom Kippur because he was fasting, praying, and asking forgiveness for all his sins. I was praying, too, but because I was little, Mama would sneak me brown paper bags inside of which were breads, fruits, and candies to keep me going throughout the day.

"You're my everything," I whispered to Mama, holding on to her tight.

She was happy then. Her shoulders were high, her cheeks full of color, her dark-brown eyes dancing. "I love you more than life itself," I told her.

I woke up from this dream, startled, breathing heavily, my mother's face finally etched clearly in my mind. I sat and remembered the creases around her eyes, the tiny dimples that revealed themselves when she smiled, the curve of her back, like she was there in front of me. I hadn't seen her face since the night Chaim took me from the ghetto to work at HASAG. But now, even the feeling of her seemed to linger in the room, floating around me.

I sat for a long while, listening to the sounds of morning: the birds outside my window, a car backfiring on the street, the chatter wafting up from the first floor as the staff prepared breakfast. For the first time in a long time, I felt safe. Mama was around me.

Henri and Jacques shooed their mother out of the apartment, pushed aside the furniture, and set up the phonograph they'd borrowed from a neighbor.

They played music they said was from America, swing music. I watched as Henri and Jacques danced, mesmerized by how their feet moved so fast and their arms and legs swung. Swing dancing was very different from the ballet I'd watched with Jane, and I sighed, relieved that the dances Henri and Jacques went to and that I would take Aurore to didn't involve classical music.

When Jacques and Henri each took one of my arms and had me follow them, I tripped over my feet and hit Henri in the nose when I tried to swing my arms. After about an hour,

I flopped down on the couch, saying it was hopeless. "I'm going to make a fool of myself in front of Aurore." I laughed.

Henri sighed, lounging back beside me. "It will take time. But you will get it. Did you ever dance in Poland?" he asked. I thought back to my brothers' bar mitzvahs and weddings, including Chaim and Golda's.

"I know the hora," I said enthusiastically. Henri and Jacques fell to the floor, holding their stomachs, laughing.

"Don't do the hora at a French dance," Henri managed to get out.

Jacques put some French music on the phonograph that he had also borrowed from the neighbor, a non-Jewish woman who had watched over their apartment while the family was in hiding. The woman had moved in her adult son to make sure no one else took the place and had given it back when Rose had returned.

Jacques played Charles Trenet, then Mireille Mathieu and after that Maurice Chevalier, Yves Montand, and Édith Piaf. I thought of Jane then and all the celebrities she had introduced me to, their names I couldn't remember except for the American actor Tyrone Power. I remembered the lunches we had with him clearly: he was movie-star handsome and reminded me of Chaim. I was sure, though, I had met some of these singers, too, as their voices sounded familiar.

Back at the mansion, Salek, Joe, Marek, and I continued dancing. All of them mastered the swing dance much more quickly than I did. Salek, though, moved on to show me a few other dances, including the foxtrot and the tango, which he said were from South America. My favorite music was "Minor Swing" by Django Reinhardt. The professor and I had seen a big band perform in Paris, and I was sure they played "Minor Swing." I found myself tapping a foot to the rhythm. That's when Joe pulled me up from the couch and told me to just dance what I felt. By following his advice, slowly I began to get the hang of it.

The waltzes that Salek played on the phonograph next sent shivers through me. These seemed too complicated for me to master. And as the music played on, I remembered HASAG. The entertainment that was put on by prisoner musicians and dancers would often be German waltzes. The Nazis would sit in small makeshift theaters and watch, smoking cigars and cigarettes and drinking expensive alcohol they had shipped in from Berlin. I'd helped out sometimes, sweeping and cleaning the rooms before and after the performances. I hadn't liked the way the SS looked at the Jewish women. I didn't like the waltzes and told Salek to turn them off.

One rainy afternoon, Henri and Jacques said that the most important dance I needed to learn was a slow dance. Henri pulled me in close to him, like we were a couple. Jacques put on a recent release called *"Les Feuilles Mortes"* or "Autumn Leaves" by Yves Montand. The pace picked up throughout the song, and while I was okay at the start, I tumbled over Henri's feet when the music gained speed. Henri sighed and, pretending he was Aurore, placed his head on my shoulder. "I like you even if you can't dance," he said in a high voice, imitating a girl.

The real challenge were my lessons on how to talk to Aurore. Henri and Jacques said I was sullen a lot of the time, that I didn't talk much, that I was introverted and seemed to come across as shy and standoffish. I needed to ask Aurore about her day, to tell her how pretty she looked, to hold her hand, and most of all be interested in her stories. I had to learn to listen. As Henri and Jacques role-played different scenarios, like Aurore confiding in me the story of her parents, how she was struggling with a certain subject in school, her experiences during the German occupation of France, which I had never asked her about, I thought back to Mama and Papa and Golda and Chaim. I saw our walks along the Kamienna River and the way my father's eyes would look at Mama. I saw also how Mama's head would tilt toward Papa's. Golda and Chaim on their wedding day, their smiles and blushing cheeks. There was a gentleness and honesty that moved between them and an understanding of each other. These couples didn't need words. Everything was expressed in a glance, a blush, and a soft laugh.

And I realized then that Papa looked at me in much the same way . . . even at HASAG, even in the ghetto. He looked at me with love.

I started crying.

Inside me was a deep, hollow void where Papa was supposed to be. I realized that the ravine I felt I kept falling into was that part of me where Papa used to live. I'd gotten rid of him. He hadn't gotten rid of me.

For a moment, before my anger toward him returned, I missed him so terribly, I felt my entire insides breaking.

———————

Jane bought a dog, a poodle, which she said I could name. I chose "Tarzan."

I would walk Tarzan along the cobblestone boulevards

with drooping trees to the Seine. I now had my own room in Jane's apartment, sleeping in a four-poster bed underneath a tapestry of silks and taffetas. Tarzan slept right beside me on the floor.

Jane and I would spend hours strolling through the long hallways and spacious rooms of the Louvre, where she explained the art to me. She talked to me about how art connected us all, unified us in ways nothing else could. She laughed over lunch in the Louvre dining room about how the mind told us one thing, the heart something else, but the soul, that's where art really touches a person. "It reflects our collective experience as human beings," she said, turning more serious. "Art reveals our pain, our joys, our sorrows, sometimes that which we ourselves are refusing to see about ourselves. Most of all, art can remind us of love."

I told Jane about the painting the professor had shown me, and we talked about when I was ill. *Truth Coming Out of Her Well*. Jane knew it and explained that it was *La Vérité sortant du puits armée de son fouet pour châtier l'humanité* (Truth coming out of her well, armed with her whip, to chastise mankind). Jane then went on to talk about France, how it was moving forward, which it should, but not taking responsibility for what it did, allowing so many of the Jews to be taken by the Nazis, enslaved in the transit camps and the stadium and then sent to the camps in Germany and Nazi-occupied Poland and ultimately to death. Neighbors who took Jewish apartments, not just in France but in every country where the Nazis, like a game of checkers, had taken all the Jewish pieces and destroyed them. Head of the French Resistance during German occupation and politician Charles De Gaulle said after French liberation that we needed grandeur, not the truth: "We, who have lived the greatest hours of our History, we have nothing else to wish than to show ourselves, up to the end, worthy of France. Long live France!"

"But we cannot forget the sufferings of the past, our roles, all our roles in the suffering of others, for we all have played a part," Jane explained. "This is Truth, coming out of her well. She can only remain there for so long before she comes out, angry, vitriolic, reminding us of what we need to really do to heal and move forward." Jane was looking at me in a strange way, like she wasn't just talking about the country, its people, but also me . . . and maybe also herself.

Jane taught me how to drink tea in delicate gold-embossed china cups, to sip champagne from crystal glasses shaped like flutes, and to eat eight-course dinners in grand dining rooms with silver forks and knives. She taught me how to knot a tie and tie a silk scarf. She bought me a leather traveling bag. She then said it was because she was taking me to a film festival in Cannes, where I would meet royalty and movie stars from America. "John Wayne?" I asked eagerly.

"Possibly," she replied.

Memory is funny, Dr. Robert Krell told me many years later. At that time with Jane, I was learning to compartmentalize, to put away somewhere Leah's struggles in Palestine, that the rest of my family members were still missing, that I was alone.

I had Henri and Jacques, Rose and Jane and her family, my boys from Buchenwald. I had a lifestyle I could never have imagined in Skarżysko-Kamienna. I might even have a girlfriend.

In late August 1947, the professor told me I had passed my exams to enter a vocational school. I was going to study to be an electrical engineer starting in January. First I had to complete some high school math and science courses.

Life, I thought, was finally good.

But niggling, chewing at me from the inside, was something I, indeed, was not looking at. I knew that Truth was trying to get me to see her, to hear her, to embrace her. She was fighting inside me to get out. I had just become a master, for a little while, of the lie.

Jane, left, and Jean seated.

Romek on vacation with Jane.

21

THE MARCHÉ DU film de Cannes.

An international film festival that had started a year earlier in the autumn of 1946.

There would be sixteen countries screening films at the 1947 festival, Jane told me and her children as we traveled by train in a first-class coach. Isabelle said we would have a chance to see some of the newest films before they even hit the theaters in Paris. The family had gone to the first festival and loved it.

Our hotel's sprawling porch overlooked the swimming pool that overlooked the Mediterranean Sea. Many of the movie stars and directors were arriving as Jane's children and I sat outside sipping lemonade. The stars of the festival came in by seaplane, and we had front-row seats as they moved their way onto boats that taxied them to docks a stone's throw away from us. The women wore tailored suits not unlike what Jane wore, with fur collars and cuffs. Smoking cigarettes set on long sticks and walking arm in arm with the men, who wore fine linen suits like those Jean wore. All the while, sailboats and water-skiers frolicked back and forth, and fans basked in the sun, emerging from the day sunburned and wind-kissed. Around me were the aromas of perfume, cigars, and the scents of the sea breeze, orange blossoms, and suntan lotion.

While Jane and Jean met up with some of the directors and producers, Isabelle, Claude, Michel, and I went off and caught *The Chase*, a dark American gangster film, followed by Walt Disney's *Dumbo*. I had never seen an animated film before and was in awe at how the drawings came to life, especially the talking elephant. I wanted to see more of these types of films Claude said were called cartoons.

As the four of us meandered back to the hotel, the palm trees swaying in a soft breeze, around us were women in ball gowns and men in tuxedos heading out to evening performances and fancy parties, some of which were taking place on the large yachts anchored in the sea.

I thought back to Buchenwald then and Jakow, wondering where he was. He had big ears, like Dumbo. He had that loping walk, long arms, was slow but deliberate in everything he did, reminding me of Dumbo. But he had confidence, where Dumbo was skittish. Jakow would belt out comedic operas, having us boys laughing for hours. He would put on skits and perform all the characters, each one with a different accent. He'd play an old failing lady, then turn around and play her saucy grandson. He would pretend to be animals, too, and we'd have to guess which ones. I learned how to play charades with Jakow in the camp. I learned how to laugh again with Jakow. As I sat with Jane and her family, listening to them talk about the films that had won awards at Cannes, I thought how Jakow, *Jakow,* in the midst of horror, risked his own life for us boys. He had used the art of storytelling, comedy, theater, and music to transport us out of our suffering, if only for a little while. That was acting and the true mark of an artist.

We remained in Cannes for a while after the festival had ended.

After lunch one day with several famous actors who had stayed as well, and an afternoon on the beach, Jane and Jean sat me down at a secluded table in a small bistro on a dead-end street. The waiter served oysters and for me a hamburger. We had Château Lafite Rothschild, a robust wine, nothing like Kiddush wine. Jane said Château Lafite Rothschild was one of the best wines in France and owned by her neighbor's family, the Rothschilds. I recounted then to Jean and Jane what had happened when we boys stayed at the Château de Ferrières, which was also owned by the Rothschilds.

"Jean is my second marriage," Jane said when I was done.

I caught Jane slipping a hand into Jean's. He looked over at Jane with that look of love I had remembered with Papa and Mama, Golda and Chaim. "I can't have any more children," Jane pressed on. "And all my children, whom I love so much, are from my first marriage. Jean and I . . ." She trailed off, her throat catching like she was about to cry.

"We have come to be very fond of you, Romek, like you are our family," Jean said.

"My children think of you as a brother," Jane added.

"I didn't think I was even likable," I said in a low voice.

"Real family," Jane continued, reaching over and holding one of my hands now. I could feel she was shaking. "We want you to be part of our family, our real family." I looked into her eyes. They were swollen with tears. Jane was usually composed. She would walk in a room as if she owned it and likely she did. She was confident and self-assured, like no woman I had ever met before. Now she was weeping.

I knew I was staring, unblinking, at Jane, uncertain where this was going and surprised to see her, for the first time, looking weak and vulnerable.

"I'm not able to have any more children," she repeated. She opened her mouth, her upper lip trembling, but nothing came out.

Jean cleared his throat. "We'd like to adopt you," he said, taking my other hand. "Do you know what that means?"

My eyes moved from Jane to Jean. He was foggy-eyed. He was the quieter of the two, usually the one to follow Jane. I looked back at Jane, who seemed to be sinking in her chair. She gripped my hand even tighter.

With his free hand, Jean pushed toward me a box with a red ribbon tied around it. I let go of their hands and opened it slowly. Inside was a gold chain pocket watch, similar to what Papa would wear.

"Will you be our son?" Jean asked. "Will you become Romek Brandt? That's what adoption means. You will become our child."

I swallowed hard, my thoughts pounding and pushing at one another.

I wouldn't be going back to Poland. I wouldn't be going to

Palestine with Leah. I would be living in Paris with Jane and Jean and their children in a palace apartment?

"D-do you want me to change my name?" I finally stammered.

Jean and Jane nodded. "You will want for nothing," Jane said, composing herself. She sat up straight and pushed her chest out the way she usually sat. "We can never replace your own family, but we can love you like our son. I would want this for one of my children if . . ." Her voice failed. She was shrinking again. "If," she started a second time, "if I was lost, I'd want someone to love them as much as I do."

"But I don't know that my family is lost," I said quickly, looking down. I knew Jane's use of the word "lost" meant "dead."

"Okay, until we find them," Jane assured me. She took my hand again and squeezed it hard. "And then we will do everything in our power to help them, too."

I asked Jane and Jean a series of questions.

Could I continue to see Henri, Jacques, and Rose?

"Of course. Whenever you like," said Jean, who was, for the first time since I met him, taking control of the conversation.

"If we find my parents or any family, can they move to France with me? Because Poland, our home . . ." I drifted off then. I didn't want to think about Poland and other people living in our house.

"Yes," Jane and Jean said at the same time.

"And I can still go to school?"

Jane and Jean laughed then. "And university and anywhere you want to go. We will support you."

"I can still see the professor . . . Professor Manfred?"

"He is part of you?" Jean asked.

I nodded.

"Then he's part of us, too," he added.

"Can I have my friends from the mansion, Salek, Joe, and Marek, sleep over?"

"Yes," Jane said with a smile. "Yes to all. I'd like the boys to spend more time at the apartment."

Thinking of Salek, Joe, and Marek in my big room at Jane and Jean's place, playing catch with Tarzan in the *parc*, talking all night long, made me smile.

"Maybe even go to America and visit Abe in New York sometime?" I quickly added, not wanting to forget him.

"We would be honored to take you," Jean said.

"I love America," Jane then cooed.

Romek Brandt. I would be Romek Brandt. I didn't sleep for two days, thinking of what my life would be like as Romek Brandt. I asked myself, "What is in a name? What does a name mean?"

"117098," I told the man sitting behind the desk.

The cattle train had arrived at Buchenwald. Abe, the other men, and I had to stand in lines outside, waiting, as one by one, we submitted our identification documents.

I kept my head down, averting my eyes both out of practice—survival meant not drawing attention to yourself, and that meant not looking into the eyes of the SS—and hoping the man behind the desk wouldn't notice my facial burns. I caught the date on a piece of paper on the desk. February 3, 1945. My birthday was the day before. I was now fourteen.

I handed the man my identification card that listed my number, that I had been a worker at HASAG, and that I was Jewish.

My eyes still on the ground, I studied the man's shiny black boots. Since Częstochowa, I was forced to wear wooden shoes or clogs, which gave my feet blisters and got stuck in the mud.

The man reviewing my documentation grunted for me to stand to the side. I opened my mouth to protest. The men who had registered before me had been sent away, probably to shower. Why was I being asked to wait?

Abe was asked to wait with me. Why? Surely they weren't going to kill him, too. He had been a foreman for one of their German factories, able to direct workers better than any man.

Abe and I huddled as close together as we could without touching, for we knew kapos, *who were the Jewish police of the camps, and the SS didn't like prisoners being close. My entire body was shaking. We were both about to die.*

When the man behind the desk had finished registering everyone, he turned to Abe and me. "I'm keeping your documents for a bit," he said in a deep, gruff voice. I wanted to look up and see his face, study his eyes, see if he was kind or lying. But I dared not. "Follow me."

From the back, I could see he was wearing a blue uniform with a black beret. I had never seen these clothes before on a German soldier or police officer. But I told myself, I had never been in Germany before. They probably had new and maybe even more brutal police units here than the SS. I couldn't feel my legs, my hands, my head. I wasn't even sure if I was walking or if all of this was a dream. I know my heart raced.

235

I knew enough moving from camp to camp that the Nazis liked kids to be sixteen or older to work. They felt anyone younger wasn't strong or healthy enough to do the jobs. If a prisoner couldn't work, they were considered useless and killed. Plain and simple. I started rambling, mumbling, stammering to the man, I think, maybe to the air, that I was a good worker. I had put insignia on the guns for HASAG and was faster than all the others, the men who did the same job.

"We're older than our papers say," I heard Abe spit out. "We're older than we look. Please . . . we can work." He was begging.

The man turned. I stopped and jumped. He sighed and leaned in close. With a finger to his mouth, telling us to shush, he said: "It's all right. Just follow me. You're safe here."

While Jean and Jacques prepared the documents for my adoption, they felt it would be best if I remained at Le Vésinet with my friends and continued my studies with the professor.

On Fridays, I would head to Champagne and Shabbat dinners with Henri, Jacques, Rose, and Hannah. At a local high school, in a class with teens my age, I studied advanced mathematics, problem solving, data processing, and some physics, preparing myself for the engineering program I was to start in January. To make sure I didn't fall behind, the professor continued to tutor me every day.

But while I did all this, at the oddest times, like in the shower or in the middle of reading a passage of a book, I'd hear Jakow's voice. Not his real voice but a memory of a conversation we'd had at Buchenwald. "You may be all that is left," he had said near liberation, when it was the most dangerous at the camp, for the Nazis wanted to kill any remaining Jews to hide their crimes from the world. "You have to survive," he had said. "You are the future."

Another time, I heard Madame Minc when she had asked me early on: "What do you want for the future, Romek? Do you know what a future is?"

And then I recalled the professor when he would ask me: "What would your parents want for you?"

"All Abram ever did was help people, including me," I shouted into the wind. "He will never get married or have a family. He will never live."

I wanted that for him.

But what did I really want for me?

Romek and Ralph with Tarzan.

22

I HAD JUST started at HASAG. It must have been the winter of 1942.

A friend from cheder, *an older boy named Schmiel, was working on the same factory floor as I was.*

His job was to run these big, heavy machines, driven by rubber belts that would wear out. When they did, the rubber was thrown in the garbage.

One day, Schmiel picked up a piece of the broken rubber, cut it into further pieces, and handed it out among us. "Put it inside your shoes," he whispered. Our shoes, at that time, were our own. But they were wearing down because no one had enough złoty for food from the black market, let alone new shoes. The rubber lined the places in our shoes where there were holes, Schmiel said.

An SS man caught Schmiel with the rubber.

That SS man, who had a mustache and must have been about six foot four, lined up all the workers in Schmiel's area and had us stand in a circle, with him and Schmiel in the middle.

"No one steals from the Third Reich," the SS man barked out. "No one!"

He then whipped out his revolver, so fast that the silver of the pistol, shimmering as it moved in the air, looked like a giant fly.

Schmiel was shot in the forehead. He stood for a moment, his eyes unblinking, the gun wound slowly seeping, like an inkblot.

When Schmiel fell to the ground, I was sure I was next, because I had some of the rubber tucked in a pocket.

I lived, though. The SS man didn't realize that Schmiel had given others part of the rubber.

But I knew then that life under the Nazis came with certain conditions. Follow the rules, all the rules; stay quiet; stay healthy; do the work; live. There was no room for mistakes.

That was the day I forgot my name, wiped it from memory until the American Army man asked me my birth name.

That was the day I became my number.

———

Salek, Joe, Marek, and I were the only ones left in our dorm room. All the other boys had left, either taking their own apartments in the city after having found jobs or moving to other countries to join relatives. Since we left Buchenwald, none of us spoke about the camp. But on this one night, with a fall wind rustling the leaves outside our window, the electric lights flickering on and off from a storm, we found ourselves reminiscing about the past.

Buchenwald, Salek reminded us, had been set up in 1937

as a camp for political prisoners and criminals. Statistics making their way to France, broadcasted over the radio and written about in news stories, reported that nearly a quarter of a million prisoners had passed through Buchenwald's front gates. There were sub-camps, too, surrounding Buchenwald, like the points of a star. A medical facility had been set up at the camp, testing vaccines for typhus and other illnesses on prisoners. Sometimes the experiments were so harsh, prisoners died or went into comas, and they didn't wake up. They'd be buried, sometimes alive.

Buchenwald inmates were slave laborers as well in a nearby munitions factory that made, among other things, components for rockets and the panzer, Germany's high-tech army tank. While the camp didn't have gas chambers, more than 55,000 prisoners were killed at Buchenwald, the media estimated, as a result of starvation, medical experiments, being worked to death, or from disease and illness.

When the Soviet Union's Red Army moved back into Poland in 1944, the Nazis started to destroy evidence of the genocide they had committed. Many Jews and other inmates were sent on death marches, where they walked until they died. Some of the death camps were set on fire, records destroyed. But prisoners still capable of working were moved into Germany. This included men of working age and boys.

When the transports from the Polish death camps started to arrive with Jewish boys like me, beginning in the spring and summer of 1944, the underground at Buchenwald was shocked. The barrack of Polish Jewish brickmasons, some of whom worked for the underground, and other Jewish Poles, including Jack Werber and that infamous Gustav, devised an intricate plan to dupe the Nazis. They told the Nazis that they wanted to set up schools for us boys where we would learn the German language, German order, and how to be good German workers. They assured the Nazis that such schools would keep us boys still and quiet, not running around the camp, stealing food and causing problems. In some cases, the underground who oversaw the transport of arrivals falsified boys' documents, giving some Christian names and stating they were Communists, not Jews. They also placed on our identification papers a note that we were not to be sent out to work. While the goal of the resistance movement at Buchenwald was to defy and eventually overthrow the Nazis, Gustav and Jack convinced the underground of the importance of making it a priority to save us Jewish boys.

In Jack's case, as Jakow told me, it was because he had discovered that his wife and daughter, who was fourteen months in 1939 when Germany occupied Poland, had been murdered. His family, including his parents, brothers, and sisters had been sent to Treblinka. But before they were killed, they also believed Jack to be dead. The Nazis had played a cruel joke on Jack's family, sending them the ashes of another man, claiming it was Jack. "They were more than cruel," Joe spat out. "The Nazis, they, not us, were the inhuman ones. They're the rats and worm food."

I had not seen Joe worked up before. He was squeezing his knuckles so tight, they turned white.

Jack himself wanted to die, Salek continued. "When he heard about his family from another prisoner . . . until we boys arrived, he debated killing himself." At a meeting to discuss the fate of the boys, Jack had said, "We agreed that if the accounts of what was happening to European Jewry were true, then it was crucial that we do something positive and important . . . Our task was to save their lives and to give them hope for the future."

The underground was able to do this because they had positions of power in the camp. In the early 1940s, as the number of inmates at Buchenwald grew, the Nazis became too small in number and, as the war progressed, too consumed with their own survival to run the camp on their own. They needed inmates to work for them. Initially, the SS sought out the criminals at Buchenwald but soon discovered that giving murderers and thieves responsibilities only increased the crime at the camp, including crimes against the Nazis. The SS had no alternative but to seek the support of the Communists, who played a game, a dangerous game, pretending to do the work but all the while being involved in subversive activities.

The Buchenwald underground or resistance, as they were also called, often didn't know who one another were in order to protect their activities and one another. They would steal extra food for children and sheltered them as best they could. The Jewish brickmasons built the Gustloff-Werke armament factory in 1943, where many of the inmates worked as slaves. It was bombed in August 1944 before I got to Buchenwald. There were lots of farms, too, in the surrounding countryside where inmates worked. And of course there was the internal operation: laundries, kitchens, and clothing warehouses where items stolen from arrivals were sorted. To oversee all these activities, the underground convinced the Nazis in 1942 to create an internal police force, most of whom worked for the underground, but the Germans didn't know that. The police force was in charge of the trains and the arrivals. These men wore the blue uniform with the beret.

After my dowsing with disinfectant, the man overseeing Abe and me gave us our documents back. These now said I was a political prisoner, a Communist, and gave my age as sixteen. The yellow star on my pajamas was replaced by a red one. The underground even operated the office.

The Nazi Party agreed to the idea of the schools in the barracks. For one, they were known for kidnapping children that they deemed German- or Aryan-looking enough and could be further Germanized. The Nazis didn't know that many of us were Jewish nor that the brickmasons were sneaking into the barracks to teach Yiddish songs and history as well as geography and math. My barrack used to be a dorm for the sick. Surrounding it was a metal fence and a gate. Jakow could hear the squeaky gate opening and knew when Nazis were approaching. In Block 66, barrack leader Antonin told the SS that typhus was spreading and not to go near the building.

The leaders of the blocks with the largest concentration of children also convinced the Nazis in charge of their barracks to allow roll call inside for the boys, instead of on the *appell-platz*, saying we boys were the future of the Nazi Party. We couldn't get sick, and winters were cold in Germany.

When more and more boys arrived, the so-called "children's" barracks weren't enough to contain us all. Boys were placed in the brothels, hidden by the women the Germans used and abused. Children were also sent out to sub-camps.

When the Nazis said the boys had to work, the underground placed us as best they could in kitchens where it was warm.

The underground got us extra food, blankets, and warm clothes. As Jack Werber said: "Suffering a great personal loss drove me in my obsession to save children. I saw each one of them as if he were my own."

The four of us cried. For the first time, as a group, we told one another our experiences. We held hands. Salek snuck away at one point, returning with a bottle of cognac that we passed around. I got drunk for the first time, too, my head swaying, the tears pouring out of me.

"For nearly a year," I said at one point, breathing heavily, remembering, remembering, how I would stand by the window staring out, waiting for Papa and Abram to return. "So many faces I saw, marching, I would stop, open my mouth to let out a small cheer, seeing Chaim, Motel, Abram, Moishe, Papa . . . even in the female guards, I'd stop. The way one stood or held her head, I'd flinch to move to her, to fling my arms around her, thinking, *Mama, Leah* . . . Then she'd turn. And it wasn't her. It was never anyone I knew. Ever. I eventually just stopped looking, the pain inside my chest, the tightening, the plunging, too much to bear."

All of us that night punched pillows, tore at our hair, scratched our legs, got angry, really angry. By the time we heard the rooster make its first morning call, the four of us dazed and lost but having gotten a lot out of us that we had cemented inside, we crawled our way to our dorm rooms, where we slept for an entire day.

———

I was spending the weekend with Jane at her apartment when Ralph came to visit.

Madame Minc had told him where I was.

I buzzed him into the building using the intercom. Ralph whistled when he walked into the large foyer with its black-and-white-checkered marble floor and large gold-framed mirror.

"Pretty nice place!" he exclaimed.

Ralph seemed different. For one, he wasn't dressed in head-to-toe black. He was wearing a dark-gray blazer over top-pleated matching pants, a white cotton shirt, and a tie. His hair was curly, not slicked back, and without all the gel, it looked lighter, not jet-black. He also didn't exude that cocky confidence. He seemed almost jittery, like he was nervous. He wouldn't look Jane in the eye when they met. "Can we go for a walk?" he mumbled to me, wringing his hands. I slipped on my black patent-leather shoes Jane had bought me, got Tarzan's lead, and called my poodle.

Outside, Ralph lit up a cigarette and passed the packet to me.

"I don't smoke," I said with a chuckle. "I never got the hang of it."

We walked toward the Seine.

"Are you not going to bug me about Jane?" I finally asked. "I know she represents everything you dislike."

"I'm going to Canada," he said, ignoring my question.

I stopped then, turning to look at him. He shrugged, knowing my question before I even asked it. "There's nothing in Eastern Europe for me," he said.

He tilted his head up toward the sky. It was an overcast

day. The low horn from a barge on the river made its way toward us. A group of young schoolchildren, the girls in pigtails and the boys in French berets, skirted past us, giggling, holding umbrellas.

"I was wrong. I mean . . . I dunno . . . what to believe," he continued after the children were gone. Ralph's speech was choppy. This wasn't Ralph, the great orator I knew.

"What about the Red Army and Stalin?" I asked.

"I think right now, I want to find peace," he said in a low, strained voice. "I want to stop fighting, not just outside but inside." He tapped his head then. "I have been waging a battle inside me of all I have seen and experienced. It was easier to forget that and fight for something else than overcome my own demons."

I nodded slowly. Even though he wasn't speaking literally, I understood, much the way I understood Elie when he spoke.

The rain got stronger. I suggested to Ralph that we head to La Mère Catherine, where everyone now knew me. The staff would let me tie up Tarzan underneath the canopy where patrons could sit outside, watching passersby while sipping their lattes. The restaurant even had dog treats and a silver bowl for water ready for Tarzan.

Ralph, though, wouldn't move.

Tarzan pooed. I took a tiny bag from my pants pocket and picked it up, the way Jane had shown me, to throw it in the garbage later.

"Whatever it is you believe in," he finally said, his gaze drifting over the river, "it has to come from the soul. Not the heart that fuels passion and sometimes is blind or the mind that tries to rationalize things. The soul. The Communists at

Buchenwald, they didn't help us because of their political beliefs. They helped us because they were good people."

Ralph and I began walking again toward La Mère Catherine. As we did so, I thought of Jakow, the Jewish brickmasons, and the Communists at Buchenwald. They saw goodness in people. Gustav did, too, even though he'd taken it into his own hands to decide good people from bad people and dole out the punishment for the latter. "You're right," I said in a hushed voice. "It was that quality of goodness and not the Communist politics that saved me, saved us."

"And Papa," I continued after we ordered our breakfast. "He believed that the Germans would do no harm to us. I blamed him . . ." I didn't know where the words were coming from, but I felt comfortable speaking to Ralph as he listened patiently. I was struck by this, too, because he seemed to be a person who liked to talk, not hear. "Maybe he wasn't the fool I thought he was," I picked up. "Maybe he isn't to blame for what happened to me, to Abram . . . to the family. Papa, in his soul, saw people as good."

And that's when I remembered something else I had locked away. In the early days of my working at HASAG, I'd stumbled during roll call, weak-kneed and feeling faint, unused to the small portions of food and the long hours of work. A Jewish *kapo* pointed at me, ordering me to get into the wagon—the large wooden wheelbarrow that was pushed around the HASAG barracks collecting the sick and dying. My hands were bloodied and wrapped in torn material from my shirt, for the calluses had not formed yet. Papa chased after the wagon, arguing with the *kapo* that I was contributing to the German war machine. Papa begged that my life be spared, for all of us knew, even then, that leaving in the wheelbarrow meant death. Papa offered to give the man złoty, jewels, anything to save my life. The *kapo* stopped, clicked his tongue, and yelled at me to get out. "I don't want anything from you, old man," he said to my father. "Get the boy food and fix his hands. Make him strong, because there might not be a next time."

"Thank you, thank you," Papa kept repeating as he folded me into his arms. He thanked the man, bowing, the way he would when reciting prayers, as the *kapo* moved off.

"People are inherently good, Romek," he whispered to me as we walked back to the barrack. "We all want one thing and that is love. Whatever happens to you, don't forget your goodness. Don't forget others' goodness. You can create great works of art, be educated, be advanced in many ways, have a great life, but if you forget goodness, then you are really suffering in this world. Don't let the Nazis take that away from you."

———

"Do you not like Jane?" I asked Ralph as we headed back to the apartment. The rain had stopped, but the sky was still dark and cloudy. "You seemed uncomfortable meeting her."

Ralph sighed. "No. I'm embarrassed. She might not even know, but I do, that I called for outright war against people of her class. She's not the problem. It's people like Hitler who abuse their power . . . they're the problem."

"When do you leave for Canada?" I asked, changing the subject.

"In a few weeks."

"What is it like, this place Canada?" I had no idea even where Canada was. At Buchenwald, when the Jewish brick-mason who taught geography came to our barracks, he'd bring with him a miniature globe that he said he had managed to have someone smuggle out for him from the storage room. He said at Auschwitz, there was a section called *Kanada*, where Jewish inmates, mostly women, would sort through the Jewish suitcases and linings of clothes, taking anything of value, including gold fillings from teeth the Nazis had pulled.

"It can be cold there," Ralph said. "But a great ocean separates Canada from Europe. If another war happens, I'll be far away."

"So it snows?" I asked, thinking of tobogganing down the sloping hills in Skarżysko-Kamienna with Motel, Moishe, and Abram.

"A lot."

"And there are lakes? Lakes to swim in and skate on?" I asked, thinking of the tire swing Chaim would attach to the long branch of an oak tree and which my brothers used to jump into the Kamienna River in the summers. I was scared of water then, of swimming. But now the thought of lakes I could bathe in during hot summers excited me.

"Yes."

"And girls?" I couldn't believe I asked that.

Ralph chuckled. "Lots of girls, and good-looking ones, too."

"Hmm," I hummed. "Hmm."

———

On every second or third Thursday of each month, the fore-man on my floor at HASAG would send me to the main office to pick up the bills of lading. There was a woman there, a secretary. She had straw-blond hair, worn short with waves. She was tall and thin. She wouldn't look at me when she passed me the pile of documents. She'd hiss at me not to lose any of the papers or mess them up and to hurry back to the main floor. "*Raus. Raus,*" she'd snap, ordering me to get lost, to leave.

But every time that woman passed me the bundles of papers, inside them, wrapped in newsprint, was a slab of thick, crusty, fresh bread and a tiny jar of marmalade.

I thought of this woman as I waved goodbye to Ralph, watching him walk down the block, making his way to the train station. I thought of her as I asked Jane and Jean if I could speak with them.

I also thought of this woman when I closed my eyes and told Jean and Jane how much they meant to me, that their kindness helped make me feel like a human again. I told Jean and Jane that they were torches in my life, like Leah had said would find me. "And you did. You found me," I said. "But you see," I started, "I think, maybe to survive, maybe because it hurt so badly to be so alone, I pushed memories of Papa and my family away. I wanted to blame Papa for everything that happened to me . . . to us. But I have come to see now that it was me trying to cut him out, not the other way around. I guess it was just too painful to remember where I came from and who I was because it was all gone. I forgot who I was.

"I was angry with Papa for so long," I added. "I didn't see him, see his love, even accept his love, in the end. But I see him now. Chil Wajsman. That was his name. And he lives on inside me."

I didn't want to be adopted. "I have to find my own way in life, follow the journey Papa had wanted for me, that I want for myself," I told Jean and Jane. I wanted to go to another country and be true to where I came from, my birth name, my religion, drawing on the love and values that my parents gave me. What Jane and Jean were offering, I added, was a dream come true for so many boys lost and orphaned. But I had been found. I finally knew who I was.

"I am Romek Wajsman. I was born and raised in Skarżysko-Kamienna, Poland. I was brought up in a Jewish community of faith and love and helping each other. I was brought up knowing and giving love."

23

"I'm sorry, but I don't want to be an emperor. That's not my business. I don't want to rule or conquer anyone. I should like to help everyone—if possible—Jew, Gentile—Black man—white. We all want to help one another. Human beings are like that. We want to live by each other's happiness—not by each other's misery. We don't want to hate and despise one another. In this world there is room for everyone. And the good earth is rich and can provide for everyone."

—*Charlie Chaplin, from* The Great Dictator

I APPLIED TO emigrate to Australia. But for some reason, Canada resonated most with me. I liked the idea of snow and that Canada's natural environment was a lot like Poland's.

Canada, Madame Minc said, had opened its immigration to accept about a thousand Jews from what was now being called the Holocaust, including boys like me. Canada, however, raised questions inside me. During World War II, about nine hundred Jews escaped the European continent on the *Motorschiff St. Louis*. The United States and Canada denied the boat to port, even though there were citizens in both countries saying they would take in the Jews. The *St. Louis* eventually returned to Europe. Some European countries accepted some of the passengers as refugees, but most ended up in the death camps. The *St. Louis* had been called the "voyage of the damned." Canada, like Poland, had quotas on the number of Jews who could study at universities. It also limited and restricted immigration of Jews. "But maybe this is to be my journey next," I told the professor one day, "not so much to go to a country where I'd be safe but to go to a country to help people understand, we Jews were not the enemy, and love is stronger than hate."

Jean and Jane agreed with my decision about the adoption, although they were heartbroken. Jane became my godmother. Jane and I continued to go to the movies, the ballet, and the opera. As a surprise, she took my cousins and me to *The Great Dictator* with Charlie Chaplin. It really was as good as Leah and Abram had said. I immediately wrote Leah and told her and Abram all about the film and what it meant to me.

Isabelle, Claude, Michel, and I remained close friends, too. I spent several weeks with the family at their summer home in Switzerland, a curved country manor that overlooked Lake Geneva, playing chess with Claude and hide-and-seek in the woods with Isabelle and Michel. Many nights, we kids built a large bonfire outside, roasted chestnuts and popcorn, and watched the fireflies dance in the woods.

The fall and winter of 1948, I spent a great deal of time with Aurore. We went to not just one but several dances. I told her, though, that we could only be friends. While I felt I could love her, inside me I knew there was someone else and she felt the same way about me. She said that her *maman* used to tell her, "Every person who comes into your life is a gift. Greet them like you are meeting yourself." Another person who spoke in riddles, I said with a laugh.

Aurore admitted that when she saw me on the train, she felt she knew me from somewhere. I confessed, I was drawn to her for the same reason. "Maybe we saw each other in our dreams." She giggled.

In the spring of 1948, I told Madame Minc and the professor that I was ready to accept that my family did not survive. One Friday at Le Vésinet, I invited Jean and Jane and their children for dinner, as well as Henri, Jacques, Rose, and Hannah. With the cooks, Hannah made a meal similar to what Mama would serve during Shabbat. That night, we performed the Kaddish for Salek's, Marek's, Joe's, and my families.

In my head, I added a special prayer asking Azrael, the angel of death, to make sure to take my family directly to heaven, to watch them on that voyage through the cloudy film that separates this life from the eternal, and that they and all those who died during the Holocaust be remembered for their honest hearts.

———

My dream of returning to my home in Skarżysko-Kamienna, that dream that kept me alive through the Holocaust, was just a dream reminding me of love, the love inside and all around me, that in my darkest days I had forgotten. My home was the love my family showered on me, and the love I have for them is eternal.

Dr. Robert Krell, Elie Wiesel, and Romek (Robbie Waisman).

Epilogue

ROMEK IMMIGRATED TO Canada in November 1948. Professor Manfred Reingwitz accompanied Romek to the ship.

Upon arrival in Canada, Romek changed his name to Robert (Robbie) Waisman. He was seventeen years old.

Since he knew French, Robbie had wanted to settle in Montreal, but the sponsoring organization, the Canadian Jewish Congress, sent him to Calgary instead. In Calgary, Robbie learned English, alongside working in one of the country's top hat-manufacturing companies. Like his time in France, Robbie was blessed with people who came into his life right when he needed them, giving him sanctuary and love. This included the Goresht family, who provided Robbie with room, board, and a Canadian family and identity. Through his work at the hat company, Robbie saved enough money to start a university engineering program, fulfilling his brother Moishe's dream. Robbie dropped out after a year, however, because he wanted to use his tuition money to bring Leah; her husband, Abram; and their child, Michael, to Canada.

They were struggling greatly in what was then Israel. Later on, he also sponsored Henri and Jacques to come to the country, supporting them until they found their own way. In Canada, Leah and Abram gave birth to a second child, whom they named Nathan.

Robbie continued working and studying for his accounting degree part-time. In 1958, through a blind date, he met his soul mate and wife, Gloria Lyons. Gloria, from Saskatchewan, was studying science at university in Alberta at the time. The couple settled back in Saskatchewan, where together they opened what became a chain of children's clothing stores. In Saskatchewan, they started their family. First born was Arlaina Joy in 1962 and then Howard Steven in 1964. The family moved to Vancouver in 1977, when Robbie branched out to become a hotelier. The family has lived in Vancouver ever since.

In Canada, Robbie spoke little, including to his own children, about his Holocaust experience, not wanting to upset them and wanting to put it behind him, although a day never passed when he didn't think of his loved ones who had been murdered by the Nazis or who were still missing, including Nathan, Motel, and Moishe. However, in 1984, when Robbie heard news reports that an Alberta schoolteacher, James Keegstra, had been teaching his students that the Holocaust was a fraud and a conspiracy made up by Jews, he felt he needed to come forward. It was then that he remembered the voices that would reach out to him in the dark at the camps, saying that if he lived, he "must tell the world what you have witnessed." With the Vancouver Holocaust Education Centre, which he cofounded with Dr. Robert Krell, an event was organized in which Robbie, one of the first Buchenwald child survivors to speak publicly, chronicled his experiences as a child during the Holocaust.

Robbie went on to become a beloved and recognized international speaker, often talking alongside Leon Bass, an African American serviceman, who was with the 183rd Engineer Combat Battalion that arrived at Buchenwald after liberation to provide support and needed supplies. Because of his activism, Robbie has received numerous humanitarian awards, including, in 2013, the Canadian Governor General's Caring Canadian Award. And in 2018, Robbie received an honorary doctorate of law from the University of Victoria.

Robbie has become a mentor for other survivors of genocide, including from Rwanda. He is also an Honorary Witness to the First Nation Truth and Reconciliation Commission, which was established in 2008 to look at the long-term impacts of the Canadian Indian residential school system on indigenous Canadians and their families.

Robbie enjoys speaking to high school students, particularly those of First Nations. Many of the young people identify with Robbie's story of family separation and alienation from culture and heritage. They particularly find value in his story, as written above, about how he found meaning to go on in the face of the worst of atrocities.

When Robbie is not traveling and speaking, he enjoys spending time with his relatives and expanding family, especially his two grandchildren, Ava and Kira. He remained close with Jane and Jean for the rest of their lives and is still close with their children and now grandchildren.

About the OSE

Jewish intellectuals and doctors in St. Petersburg, Russia, founded the Œuvre de Secours aux Enfants (OSE) in 1912. The organization then was called *Obshchestvo Zdravookhraneniia Yevreyev* (the Organization for the Protection of the Health of the Jewish Population, or OZE). The original mandate of the OZE was to provide medical treatment to Jewish communities that survived Russia's massacre of the Jews, known as pogroms.

Following the Bolshevik Revolution, also referred to as the Russian Revolution, in 1917, the OZE moved to assisting Jewish communities in Poland and other eastern countries bordering Russia. In 1922, under its first president, Albert Einstein, the OZE became a network of groups working across several countries, with its headquarters in Berlin. In Berlin, the organization became known as the Union OSE.

Due to Nazi persecution in Germany, the headquarters moved again to France and took on the name Œuvre de Secours aux Enfants (OSE).

During World War II, the OSE's mission was to save Jewish children. Through intricate networks of support, the organization managed to smuggle Jewish children from other European countries to Vichy, the unoccupied zone in Southern France. There, the OSE ran fourteen children's homes, funded in large part by the United Jewish Appeal and the Joint Distribution Committee. Working for the OSE and directly in these homes were Jewish doctors, psychologists, and social workers who had been expelled from their professions and were threatened with deportation by the Nazis to death camps.

When the Nazis increased their roundup of Jews in France and took control of the Vichy territory in 1942, French Jewish families began leaving their children in the OSE's care as well. The OSE devised an intricate underground network that included falsifying documents to get the children to neutral countries, including Switzerland and Spain. It is estimated that during the war, the OSE saved more than 1,200 children.

At the end of World War II, the OSE in Switzerland received a cable from the commander of the American troops who had liberated Buchenwald: "Have found a thousand Jewish children in Buchenwald. Take immediate action to evacuate them." It took a little more than two months for the OSE to move 427 of the youngest boys from Buchenwald to France.

The Buchenwald Boys, as they came to be known, were the largest concentration of Jewish orphaned children to be found following the Holocaust. Again relying on Jewish scholars, health workers, artists, and psychologists, the OSE aimed to provide these boys with the medical and psychological care they needed to become part of society again. Part of the OSE's services to the children was matching them with mentors, usually adults, as well as schooling; language tutoring; and most importantly the fundamentals, such as hygiene, proper diet, and health care. Initially, some connected with the OSE did not think the boys could overcome their traumas and be functional within that society.

The Buchenwald Boys ended up shocking everyone.

Timeline

January 1933: Adolf Hitler, leader of The National Socialist German Workers' Party, or more commonly known as the Nazi Party, is made chancellor of Germany. The Nazi Party platform seeks to strengthen the Germanic people, referring to Germans as the Aryan master race. To protect the purity of the Aryan race, non-Aryans and Aryans viewed as inferior because of mental and physical disabilities are targeted for exclusion and eventually death. Jews and Socialists, whom Hitler perceived to control Germany, are especially targeted.

February 27, 1933: the Nazis burn Berlin's Reichstag (German Parliament), blaming it on Communists, resulting in a state of emergency and many civil liberties for German citizens being stripped away.

March 1933: the Nazis start construction of concentration camps in Germany to hold political opponents, namely Communists, criminals, and other enemies of the regime.

March 1933: due to the state of emergency, German Parliament passes an act giving Hitler dictatorial powers.

April 1933: Jewish shops and businesses are boycotted. Not long after, Jews are banned from taking part in the arts, owning land, and running newspapers.

1934: Jews in Germany are not allowed to take part in politics, have access to national health care, or act as lawyers or judges.

August 1934: the German president, Paul von Hindenburg, dies. Not long after, Hitler becomes führer of Germany, further solidifying his dictatorship and fascist regime.

September 15, 1935: the Nazi Party implements the Nuremberg Race Laws that marginalize and exclude Jews from the German state and society.

March 7, 1936: the Nazis begin their expansion plans, occupying the Rhineland in what is today Western Germany. In the Treaty of Versailles following World War I, the Rhineland was given to France to control.

March 12 and 13, 1938: Nazi troops enter Austria. Austria joins a union with Germany.

October 15, 1938: Nazi troops occupy Sudetenland, a Germanic area located along the Czech border that at the time was annexed as part of Czechoslovakia.

November 9 and 10, 1938: the *Kristallnacht*, the Night of Broken Glass, or the November Pogroms—a massacre aimed at destroying the Jewish population—takes place in Germany. More than 250 Jewish synagogues are destroyed, alongside Jewish homes, hospitals, and schools. Thousands of Jewish businesses are demolished, and 30,000 Jewish men are sent to concentration camps in Germany.

March 15 and 16, 1939: Nazi troops take over Czechoslovakia.

September 1, 1939: the Nazis invade Poland, which has the largest population of Jews in Europe at about 3.35 million.

September 3, 1939: Great Britain and France declare war on Germany but do not intervene to assist Polish forces in fighting against the Nazis.

Mid-September, 1939: in a pact made between Germany and the Soviet Union, headed by Soviet leader Joseph Stalin, Soviet troops pledge not to attack Germany in its takeover of Poland in exchange for control of Eastern Poland. The Soviet Union's Red Army invades Poland to the east. The Nazis and Soviets divide Poland between the two nations. The Nazis murder Jews and Poles who hold positions in politics, the law, and at universities as well as writers, musicians, and other artists who could organize resistance movements.

1940: Jewish quarters that came to be known as ghettos are formed in Nazi-controlled areas of Poland. Millions of Jews are forced to live in these Jewish Quarters, many of which will eventually be surrounded by cement and barbed-electrical-wire fences. Jews in Poland are denied almost all rights and must live on food rations that force them to survive on just a few hundred calories a day.

May 10, 1940: the Nazis successfully invade the Netherlands, Belgium, and France.

June 22, 1940: in an armistice between France and Germany, France is divided into a free zone in the south and a German-occupied zone in the north.

October 7, 1940: the Nazis invade Romania.

November 1940: Hungary, Romania, and Slovakia become allies of the Nazis.

Summer 1940: the *kommandant* of Auschwitz, Rudolf Höss, is informed that his concentration camp has been chosen to implement the Final Solution of the Jewish question (how to kill all Jews of continental Europe). Zyklon-B gas will be tested at Auschwitz for use in the mass murder of Jews.

Late June 1941: Hitler breaks the German-Soviet Nonaggression Pact and attacks Soviet territory, including the Soviet-occupied areas of Poland.

August 1941: the Soviet Union allows Polish citizens to fight alongside the Red Army. In the Soviet Union, the remnants of the Polish Army regroup.

January 1942: Jews from France and Slovakia are deported to Auschwitz-Birkenau, the Nazi concentration camp in German-occupied Poland.

May 1942: at Birkenau, the first "selections" of Jews take place by the Nazis. Those selected are sent to be killed.

Throughout 1942: French, Dutch, Belgian, German, Norwegian, and Croatian Jews are sent to Auschwitz-Birkenau, along with the Roma people. Jews in Poland are also transported to other Nazi death camps to be killed, including Treblinka, which opens on July 22, 1942.

January 29, 1943: the Nazis order all Roma people to be sent to concentration camps to be murdered.

March 1943: Jews from Greece are sent to Auschwitz-Birkenau to be killed.

July 9 and 10, 1943: Allied troops land in Sicily.

January 3, 1944: Russian troops, known as the Red Army, begin pushing Germany out of Poland.

March 19, 1944: Nazis occupy Hungary. Approximately 440,000 Hungarian Jews are deported to Auschwitz-Birkenau. More than 80 percent are murdered upon arrival.

June 6, 1944: D-Day, the day the Allies land in Normandy and begin their push to liberate France and then oust the Nazis from Germany.

July 24, 1944: Soviet troops, pushing against Germany from the east, liberate the first concentration camp at Majdanek.

August 1944: France is liberated from the Germans.

Throughout 1944 and 1945: as Allied forces advance in the west and the Red Army in the east, the Nazis conduct "death marches" of remaining survivors of German concentration camps in Nazi-occupied Poland. They transport to Germany those who appear healthy and able to work as slave laborers.

January 27, 1945: Russian troops liberate Auschwitz-Birkenau.

April 4, 1945: Ohrdruf, a sub-camp of the Buchenwald concentration camps in Germany, is liberated by the American Army.

April 11, 1945: the Americans liberate Buchenwald. To their astonishment, the American Army finds more than a thousand boys under the age of eighteen. These boys form the largest concentration of Jewish child survivors.

Later in April 1945: doctors brought in to Buchenwald are concerned the boys will not recover from the traumas of what they have experienced. One doctor thinks the boys, due to their fragile mental and physical health, won't live past the age of forty.

May 7, 1945: Germany surrenders.

Early May 1945: a transport of trucks with about 250 Buchenwald Boys departs for Prague, and the boys journey to their homes in Czechoslovakia, Hungary, and Romania.

June 15, 1945: the Œuvre de Secours aux Enfants, or the OSE (the Jewish children's relief organization that, during the German occupation of France, hid and rescued thousands of French Jewish children), receives the transport of 427 of the Buchenwald Boys in France. The OSE aims to rehabilitate the Buchenwald Boys, helping find surviving family and supporting those with no place to go. Later, some 250 or so Buchenwald Boys are transported to Switzerland, where the Swiss Red Cross will care for them.

Late 1940s: the mass killing of Jews is called the Holocaust and a genocide, the attempt by one group of people to eliminate through death another group of people.

Acknowledgments

There are many individuals and organizations that have inspired me to share my story. Foremost, though, this book would not be possible without the support and efforts of my late wife, Gloria, who championed me at every turn. She was the love of my life and my confidante with whom I initially shared stories of my past that I had kept hidden from the world. She emboldened me and provided me with the confidence to eventually speak. I am eternally grateful to my Gloria, and I hope she is smiling down from the heavens to see this memoir finally come to fruition. I LOVE you more than words can express.

To my children, Arlaina and Howard, I wish to express my gratitude, love, and appreciation for all your support and encouragement. And to my grandchildren, Ava and Kira, and son-in-law, Ian, and daughter-in-law, Cheryl, who have helped me with my journey into light. My life is full again with all of you by my side. I know my mother and father are somewhere smiling.

And I must thank so many people without whom I would not be here to give testimony to both the evils of mankind as well as the triumph over that evil. First off, all the boys of Buchenwald, including my closest brothers. Abe, Salek, Marek, Joe, Lulek, and all the others: our bond is unbreakable. The strength to overcome the unimaginable is a testament to our resilience. All of you are part of me and you flow through me like the blood in my veins. And to my friend Elie Wiesel, who was going to write the foreword for this memoir but unfortunately passed away in 2016. Elie was a brilliant mind whose insight, writing, and pertinent questions are to be pondered by everyone who is human. You are dearly missed.

Of course our eventual immersion back into society would not have been possible without the caring staff and volunteers at the Oeuvre de Secours Aux Enfants. The staff and many volunteers believed in us boys when few others did. One such volunteer, Manfred Reignwitz, became my angel, my mentor, who through our many conversations helped me overcome my demons and feel confident I could live again.

Thank you, Michele and Brigitte Renaud and Jane Brandt, for helping me to become human again. You provided love and support and immeasurable opportunities that I would never have experienced otherwise. I owe you a debt of gratitude. And of course Jacque and Henri Mydlorski provided friendship to me after the war, first as French boys and citizens close to me in age, and then, when I discovered they were blood relatives, my cousins. *Merci*. Without any of you, I would not be here now to tell my story.

Thank you to the Goresht family, who welcomed me into their home in Canada without my knowing a word of English and helped me start anew, a life I never could have dreamed of. I would also like to thank all the board members, staff, volunteers, and survivors connected with the Vancouver Holocaust

Education Centre, which I cofounded in 1994 with my dear friend Dr. Robert Krell. All of us together have created a lasting legacy to continue the fight against racism and toward a goal of "never again," where history will not repeat itself. It was Dr. Krell who reached out and convinced me to inoculate against hatred by speaking publicly. He arranged a platform through symposiums and lectures to reach many young minds.

And while on the subject of injustices, even my beautiful Canada, one of the most tolerant and inclusive countries in the world, has some of its own embarrassing past transgressions with the treatment of its own Aboriginal, Japanese, and Punjabi communities. The First Nations communities have invited me to share my experience with their own people as it relates to their systemic subjugation, and they have honored me too by asking me to participate as a witness for the Truth and Reconciliation Commission. This commission was set up to investigate the injustices forced upon Aboriginal youth within the Indian Residential Schools that tore apart their families and attempted to destroy their culture. They too have inspired and helped me to grow as an individual trying to shine light on darkness, and to eventually write this book.

I would also like to thank the following University of British Columbia professors, Dr. Graham Forest, Dr. Jay Eidelman, and Dr. Richard Menkis, as well as the many high school teachers across Canada and the United States, who have given me a platform to share my story with students. In making sure we do not repeat the past, we need to remember, and sadly, and increasingly as time goes on, fewer and fewer young people are aware of the Holocaust.

To Leon Bass as well, thank you. Leon was part of the African American unit of the US Army that entered Buchenwald shortly after liberation. Leon's willingness to lecture about witnessing the horrors of liberating Buchenwald combined with his own personal experience of discrimination as a Black man in America and in the US military has empowered many hearts and souls to understand that suffering and degradation are not relegated to any one color or religion.

I must also thank Steven Spielberg and the staff and the volunteers of the Shoah Foundation, diligently collecting the testimonies of survivors and taking the time to include me alongside the others.

There are so many incredible individuals l have met through the years who have joined me to share their own stories and struggles with oppression. One incredible young man that I'm thankful to have met is Eloge Butera, who at the age of ten survived the Rwanda Massacre in 1994. Like myself he suffered unspeakable loss and pain but has also found the strength to go on and thrive in Canada. His terrible experience reminded me that humanity is inclined to repeat past mistakes and the importance of messages of love and compassion to battle hatred must continue.

I would also like to thank survivor and personal friend Aron Eichler of Calgary, who provided me with inspiration early on as a Holocaust educator. I would be remiss without acknowledging the inspiration I also garnered from good friend and child survivor—and noted author—Jack Kuper, and his wife, Terry.

In 2002, the documentary film *Boys from Buchenwald* was released, produced by David Paperny Films and the National Film Board of Canada. The film traces a few of our journeys from Buchenwald to Écouis and where we eventually migrated after. Thank you to all involved for remembering.

One individual who was paramount to my breaking my

silence was a misguided high school teacher by the name of James Keegstra from Eckville, Alberta. Mr. Keegstra taught students that the Holocaust never occurred and that it was a fabrication by Jews and a conspiracy. It was with the news reports of his hateful teachings that I started to bear witness and speak publicly. In that same frame, I would like to thank Canada for recognizing that freedom of speech is an important cornerstone to democracy but that it comes with a responsibility. I am grateful I was welcomed into a country with values and morals and that misrepresenting and distorting history and truth is not without consequence. I am also grateful to Canada for opening its doors and welcoming me, and other survivors like me, to start a new life.

And last but far from least, I want to express my heartfelt appreciation to Susan McClelland for her magic in breathing life into my story. Her command of the language and her ability to paint a sumptuous picture with words is far beyond my own skill set. I am thrilled and honored that she was eager to collaborate on my memoir.

—*Robert Waisman*

This book would not be possible without our editor at Bloomsbury, Susan Dobinick, and our fabulous agents, Rob Firing in Toronto and John Richard Parker in London. Thank you for believing in Robbie's story and fighting so hard to see it told not just in North America but around the world.

Robbie and I wish to also thank Dr. Robert Krell, for his gentle pushing to ensure this story was documented and for his thoughtful and thorough review of the manuscript. We are also indebted to Professor Kenneth Waltzer, professor emeritus social relations and policy at Michigan State University and the world's foremost expert on the Buchenwald Boys. Dr. Waltzer provided crucial information to fill in the gaps where Robbie's memory, after more than seventy-five years, faltered. Dr. Waltzer also provided an important and thorough review of the manuscript for accuracy. Thank you also to Dr. Piotr Wróbel, Konstanty Reynert Chair of Polish History, Munk School of Global Affairs at the University of Toronto, who diligently worked with me to understand the complexities of Polish society under Nazi-occupied rule. And thank you also to the Œuvre de Secours aux Enfants for their access to files and generous help and for believing in the *Boy from Buchenwald* when few others did.

This book would also not be possible without the beautiful Gloria. Her memory caught and cradled Robbie in the telling of his story. Gloria is the backbone of this book, while her sister Harriet Goldenberg, a counselling psychologist, ensured that the journey from trauma to healing was reflected properly—that all of us in our wounds can find a light to guide us. To Howard and Arlaina and the entire Waisman clan, who over Gloria's delicious cooking shared their memories of their father and the incredible angels that never left his side.

Finally, thank you to the Canadian Council for the Arts for the more-than-generous financial support and their belief, too, in the importance of this story for young readers—and the importance and growing genre of young adult nonfiction and memoirs.

—*Susan McClelland*